Public Schools and Pregnant and Parenting Adolescents

A LEGAL GUIDE

Public Schools and Pregnant and Parenting Adolescents

A LEGAL GUIDE

Anne Dellinger

INSTITUTE OF GOVERNMENT
March 2004

The author expresses deep appreciation to the Institute of Government and to the Z. Smith Reynolds Foundation, the Karl and Anna Ginter Foundation, and the Mary Norris Preyer Fund for supporting research for the adolescent pregnancy project. The Z. Smith Reynolds Foundation and the Institute of Government funded printing and distribution of this publication.

www.adolescentpregnancy.unc.edu

E STABLISHED IN 1931, the Institute of Government provides training, advisory, and research services to public officials and others interested in the operation of state and local government in North Carolina. The Institute and the university's Master of Public Administration Program are the core activities of the School of Government at The University of North Carolina at Chapel Hill.

Each year approximately 14,000 public officials and others attend one or more of the more than 200 classes, seminars, and conferences offered by the Institute. Faculty members annually publish up to fifty books, bulletins, and other reference works related to state and local government. Each day that the General Assembly is in session, the Institute's *Daily Bulletin*, available in print and electronic format, reports on the day's activities for members of the legislature and others who need to follow the course of legislation. An extensive Web site (www.sog.unc.edu) provides access to publications and faculty research, course listings, program and service information, and links to other useful sites related to government.

Operating support for the School of Government's programs and activities comes from many sources, including state appropriations, local government membership dues, private contributions, publication sales, course fees, and service contracts. For more information about the School, the Institute, and the MPA program, visit the Web site or call (919) 966-5381.

Michael R. Smith, DIRECTOR
Thomas H. Thornburg, ASSOCIATE DIRECTOR FOR PROGRAMS
Patricia A. Langelier, ASSOCIATE DIRECTOR FOR OPERATIONS
Ann C. Simpson, ASSOCIATE DIRECTOR FOR DEVELOPMENT
Ted Zoller, ASSOCIATE DIRECTOR FOR FINANCE

FACULTY

Gregory S. Allison	James C. Drennan	Jill D. Moore
Stephen Allred (on leave)	Richard D. Ducker	Jonathan Morgan
David N. Ammons	Robert L. Farb	David W. Owens
A. Fleming Bell, II	Joseph S. Ferrell	William C. Rivenbark
Frayda S. Bluestein	Milton S. Heath Jr.	John Rubin
Mark F. Botts	Cheryl Daniels Howell	John L. Saxon
Phillip Boyle	Joseph E. Hunt	Jessica Smith
Joan G. Brannon	Willow Jacobson	Carl Stenberg
Mary Maureen Brown	Robert P. Joyce	John B. Stephens
Anita R. Brown-Graham	Diane Juffras	A. John Vogt
William A. Campbell	David M. Lawrence	Aimee Wall
Anne M. Dellinger	Janet Mason	Richard Whisnant
Shea Denning	Laurie L. Mesibov	Gordon P. Whitaker

Cover photograph by John W. Moses Jr. originally appeared in *The Youngest Parents: Teenage Pregnancy As It Shapes Lives* by Robert Coles et al., published by Duke University's Center for Documentary Studies in association with W. W. Norton & Company.

Contents

Preface

THIS GUIDEBOOK IS THIRD IN A SERIES explaining the law to pregnant and parenting adolescents, their parents, and the professionals who work with them. Knowing these students' options, school employees and officials should be better able to help them. Many statements made here about the law apply to anyone who is or wants to be a public school student. Most of the legal discussions, however, focus on pregnant or parenting unemancipated minor girls, and the text sometimes emphasizes the youngest girls for two reasons: They present the legal issues most starkly and arguably they are the neediest.

Terminology is an issue in this series. No single term accurately and respectfully describes all pregnant and parenting adolescents. I use both "girls" and "young women" in order to recognize the differences in age and maturity within the group. Many sources, including the American Academy of Pediatrics' Committee on Adolescence, prefer "girls." One practitioner uses it "to remind myself not to treat [pregnant adolescents] as miniature adults." Another writes, "At 13, 14, 15 and 16 years old they may be mothers, but they are not yet women." Robert Coles' book shows the range of terms.[1] The text refers to "woman," "young woman," "mother," "young mother," and "youths." One of the book's photographers almost always writes of "girls," while the other uses "teenagers," "adolescents," and "parents." Coles himself states a clear preference, which is then challenged. When a young father refers to himself, his mate, and other young parents as "boys and girls," Coles suggests to him that they are "men and women." The teen father emphatically rejects the suggestion. I have accepted the verbal dilemma as a reflection of the ambivalence that society—and I—feel about adolescent sexuality and its consequences.

1. ROBERT COLES, ET AL., THE YOUNGEST PARENTS: TEENAGE PREGNANCY AS IT SHAPES LIVES (1997).

The choice of topics for the legal guides emerged from several kinds of research. First, the co-director of the Adolescent Pregnancy Project, Arlene Davis, who is a nurse as well as a lawyer, reviewed 186 medical records of girls pregnant when under fifteen years of age and 15 medical records of infants born to them. Most of these patients had delivered at a hospital in North Carolina after receiving prenatal care at a local health department. A smaller number had an abortion performed at the hospital or, in more cases, at a private urban clinic in the state. The medical record review provided information about the medical and social problems affecting these patients during pregnancy and sometimes for years to come; hinted at the nature of their interactions with family members and service providers; and identified many legal questions professionals want answered. The records showed the young women's desire to complete school and demonstrated that some were having difficulty re-enrolling. In addition, the American Civil Liberties Union of North Carolina (ACLU-NC) surveyed school districts (112 of 117 responded) and pregnant and parenting students (81 responses) about school policies and practice and shared the information with me.[2]

Second, I researched relevant state and federal law on minors' pregnancy and parenting.

Third, Davis and I interviewed 120 North Carolinians who play some role in adolescent pregnancy and discussed particular points with many more. They included school administrators, social workers, counselors, and school nurses; state and local department of social services (DSS) directors, staff, and attorneys; nurses, nurse practitioners, physicians, and social workers in hospitals, health departments, community outreach programs, nonprofit agencies, private practice settings, and on medical faculties; maternity care coordinators; an owner, directors, and staff members of two clinics that offer abortion among other reproductive health services; a counselor in a pregnancy support center; adoption specialists; district court judges, attorneys who have represented pregnant minors seeking waivers of parental consent to abortion, and prosecutors; parents of girls who became pregnant

2. The survey was conducted between October 1999 and 2002.

as minors; court-appointed guardians for such girls; and adult women who gave birth in their midteens. To protect their privacy, we made no effort to contact pregnant girls or their partners. However, Arlene Davis observed two sessions at a teen prenatal clinic, and together we listened for fifteen hours to telephone operators as they staffed a national abortion referral line. I also saw, in person and on videotape, presentations that a dozen pregnant and parenting teens made in the Johnston County schools and answered questions about law submitted by teens enrolled in an adolescent parenting program in the Winston-Salem/Forsyth school district.

Fourth, we gathered data on facilities, programs, individuals to contact, written material, and other types of assistance available to adolescents and school staff. It is available at www.adolescentpregnancy.unc.edu under the heading "Schools' Resource List."

We do not vouch for or endorse any resource; and the book offers information, not legal advice. For legal advice, readers must consult an attorney. In addition, because the law is constantly in flux, readers or their legal advisors must check statutes or regulations cited in this guide to see whether they have been repealed or amended and must determine whether court decisions cited have been modified by subsequent decisions.

In addition to the funders previously mentioned, I deeply appreciate the collaborative contributions of the Adolescent Pregnancy Project's advisory committee and of those who reviewed drafts of this publication and who graciously talked with us or assisted the project in other ways.

Anne Dellinger
March 2004

Introduction

EACH YEAR IN NORTH CAROLINA about seven thousand women seventeen years old and younger become pregnant.[1] The great majority of them give birth and raise their babies. While each one's circumstances are unique, as a group they and their families can benefit from understanding and considerable help from school authorities. Many aspects of early motherhood are challenging and problematic. Of these, none is more important for mother, child, and future children than her ability to continue with education—to graduate from high school and whenever possible pursue higher education and vocational or career training.

Even a young woman who is mature, bright, and competent for her age will find it hard to negotiate pregnancy, then care for a child, perhaps hold a job too, and keep up with school. She—particularly if in middle school—will likely have little support from peers and in some cases from teachers. School personnel have legal obligations to these students and they have an opportunity to do more. By recognizing educational needs and showing sympathy and flexibility in addressing them, schools offer crucial assistance to this vulnerable group.

This book is written for superintendents, principals, school board members, counselors, school nurses and psychologists, social workers, teachers, administrators, and state education officials. It should also interest school attorneys.

Several types of information are presented. The book explains relatively clear legal requirements that apply to these students; offers interpretation of less-clear parts of the law; and sometimes ventures predictions about unresolved legal questions. It refers to the literature on adolescent pregnancy

---

1. The reported number was 6,615 in the latest year for which statistics are available; 4,890 of the pregnancies resulted in live births. North Carolina State Center for Health Statistics, *2002 Reported Pregnancies*, available at http://www.schs. state.nc.us/SCHS.

and relays advice from school professionals and others. The author's observations are heavily influenced by interviews with North Carolina professionals who work with pregnant and parenting adolescents as well as the review of medical records of early adolescent obstetric patients mentioned in the preface. The book's goals are to make caring for this group of students easier and to ensure that they benefit as much as possible from their schooling.

The Legal Status of Minors

SCHOOLS CAN WORK BETTER with pregnant or parenting students if school personnel know, in general, how the law affects minors. This section summarizes important legal duties and privileges of parents and minor or dependent children. A number of the topics covered are treated at greater length elsewhere in the guide.

PARENTS' RIGHTS AND OBLIGATIONS

Parents must care for and supervise their children and provide them with necessities such as food, clothing, shelter, health care, and education. They must not abuse or neglect a child nor let others do so. A parent's duties continue until the child is eighteen or otherwise emancipated.[1] Mothers and fathers share the duties equally—and they fall on minor as well as adult parents.[2] There is no minimum legal age for parenting. Unless a court rules otherwise, a minor parent retains the rights and duties of parenthood. For a person of any age, failure to carry out a parent's duties can result in civil and criminal penalties[3] and cause authorities to take custody of a child or even terminate parental rights.[4]

1. N.C. GEN. STAT. § 50-13.4 (hereafter G.S.). *See also* G.S. 14-322(d), G.S. 49-7, and G.S. 110-129(2).
2. North Carolina is unusual in requiring grandparents to support a child if one or both of the child's parents are minors and the parents together cannot provide full support. G.S. 50-13.4(b), upheld in *Whitman v. Kiger,* 353 N.C. 360, 543 S.E.2d 476 (2001). The law recognizes that, like parents, some grandparents cannot provide any support and that some can contribute more than others. The court decides how much each pays.
3. G.S. Ch. 14, Article 39, Protection of Minors, contains criminal statutes. The state court of appeals finds the same duty in civil law. Coleman v. Cooper, 89 N.C. App. 188, 366 S.E.2d 2, *discretionary review denied,* 322 N.C. 834, 371 S.E.2d 275 (1988).
4. G.S. Ch. 7B, especially Articles 3, 5, and 11.

A child's pregnancy or parenting does not relieve her parents of these duties toward her. For example, although parents can arrange for a minor child to live outside their home, they remain responsible. If, as sometimes happens when a child becomes pregnant, they ordered her to leave without arranging suitable care, the department of social services (DSS) could file a petition alleging parental neglect.[5]

Minor children, for their part, are "subject to the supervision and control" of their parents.[6] Here is an actual example related to teen parenting: A minor mother wanted to attend a hospital school to be near her infant in the neonatal intensive care unit. When her mother refused permission—also refusing to let her take the hospital's infant care class or her regular school's parenting class—the teen could not enroll in any of these.[7] Thus, although the law allows a minor to act as a parent, her range of choices is usually affected by her status as a minor.

The law describes a child of six or older who refuses parental demands as *undisciplined,* defined as someone who is "regularly disobedient," "beyond disciplinary control," "regularly found in places where it is unlawful for a juvenile to be," or who has run away for more than twenty-four hours. (Pregnant girls are overrepresented among homeless and runaway youth. They may run away because they are pregnant or become pregnant while living on the street.)[8] For anyone aged six to fifteen, the definition of undisciplined also includes being absent from school without permission.[9] Undisciplined is a less serious status than delinquent. A *delinquent* minor is one aged six to fifteen who commits a crime or infraction under state law or local ordinance.[10]

5. G.S. 7B-101(15).

6. G.S. 7B-3400.

7. Review of medical records of North Carolina girls pregnant before age fifteen. (See "Preface.")

8. Telephone conversation with Julie Bosland, Special Assistant to the Commissioner, Administration on Children, Youth and Families, U.S. Department of Health and Human Services, February 2, 2000.

9. G.S. 7B-1501(27).

10. G.S. 7B-1501(7).

EMANCIPATION

An *emancipated* person may conduct business as an adult, is no longer entitled to parental support, and is legally free of parental control.[11] Becoming eighteen is the usual means of emancipation. Younger teens can be emancipated by several means. Marriage is one.[12] Another is open only to sixteen- and seventeen-year-olds who have lived in the state for six months. They may petition a court for an order of emancipation. Lastly, a minor enrolled in the armed services is no longer "subject to the supervision and control" of parents.[13] Being pregnant or a parent does not emancipate a minor in North Carolina.

In the court proceeding for emancipation the minor must persuade the judge by a preponderance of the evidence that emancipation would be in her best interests.[14] The law assumes, although it is not always true, that the minor's parents object to her emancipation. They must be given notice of the hearing[15] and, like the minor, may present evidence and cross-examine witnesses.[16] The judge considers these questions in deciding whether to emancipate the minor:

- Do her parents need her earnings?
- Can she function as an adult?
- Does she need to be legally able to enter into contracts or to marry?
- Is she employed and does she have stable living arrangements?

11. G.S. 7B-3507.
12. G.S. 7B-3402. Some married adolescents get a divorce while they are still under eighteen. Although the law does not address their status, it is the author's opinion that such a minor remains emancipated.
13. G.S. 7B-3402. Minors must have parental permission to enlist if they are only seventeen. In effect, by consenting to enlistment, the parent assents to emancipation.
14. G.S. 7B-3503.
15. G.S. 7B-3502.
16. G.S. 7B-3503.

- Is there family discord and, if so, is parent/child reconciliation unlikely?
- Is she rejecting family supervision or support?
- How good are the supervision and support?[17]

After weighing the answers the judge is permitted to grant the petition if these conditions are met:

- All parties have had a chance to be heard.
- The minor offered a plan for adequately providing for her own needs and expenses.
- She is knowingly seeking emancipation and understands its legal effects.
- Emancipation would be in her best interests.[18]

MARRIAGE

In our state people can marry without restriction at eighteen, or earlier if emancipated through the court procedure. (See "Emancipation," above.) Otherwise, sixteen- and seventeen-year-olds need consent to marry from an adult having legal custody of them or serving as their guardian.[19] A fourteen- or fifteen-year-old girl may marry only if (1) she is pregnant or has a child by the person she agrees to marry and (2) a district court judge authorizes the marriage. Likewise, a fourteen- or fifteen-year-old boy may marry a woman he has impregnated or who is the mother of his child if he agrees to be married and a judge authorizes it.[20]

17. G.S. 7B-3504.
18. G.S. 7B-3505.
19. G.S. 51-2(a1).
20. G.S. 51-2.1(a). The form (AOC-CV-120) and instructions for an underage person to initiate the judicial process are available at www.nccourts.org/Forms/FormSearch.asp.

To authorize marriage for a fourteen- or fifteen-year-old, a judge must find that the young person can fulfill the responsibilities of marriage and that marriage would be in her or his best interest. Before ruling on "best interest," the judge must listen to the underage person's parents, custodian, guardian, and guardian ad litem (GAL) but does not have to follow their opinions. The GAL will be an attorney whom the judge asks to investigate and then advise on the minor's best interest and to assess, among other things, "the emotional development, maturity, intellect, and understanding" of the youth.[21] The minor is not entitled to appointed counsel to represent her, however. The statute specifies that the fact that a girl or woman is pregnant or has given birth is not enough to show that it is in the underage person's best interest to marry.[22]

North Carolina law strongly favors marriage and the legitimacy of children, and many pregnant and parenting teens do marry. However, teen marriages present difficult issues.[23] While each case must be considered on its own merits, the marriages of young women married before age eighteen are nearly twice as likely to end in divorce as those of women married at age

21. G.S. 51-2.1(d).

22. G.S. 51-2.1(a).

23. According to one source, a policy allowing early marriage "subordinates other interests, such as those of the parents and guardians of the underage applicant [for a marriage license] and the long-term welfare of both the child and its mother." William A. Campbell, *North Carolina Marriage Laws: Some Questions*, 63 POPULAR GOV'T 50, 53 (Winter 1998). Another legal writer points out that the Uniform Marriage and Divorce Act, which North Carolina has not adopted, allows no one younger than sixteen to consent to marriage and "expressly rejects pregnancy as an automatic exception to an age requirement" because "marriages entered into under these circumstances are even more vulnerable than other youthful marriages." SUZANNE REYNOLDS, 1 LEE'S NORTH CAROLINA FAMILY PRACTICE § 2.8 at 98 (5th ed. 1993). A third source concludes that "[a]dolescent child bearers may not be able to combine school attendance and marriage successfully." Diane Scott-Jones, *Educational Levels of Adolescent Childbearers at First and Second Births*, 99 AM. J. EDUC. 461, 477 (Aug. 1991).

twenty-five or above.[24] Marriage can have adverse legal consequences besides divorce. For example, marriage may relieve a person under sixteen of the legal obligation to attend school. (See "Compulsory Attendance," below.) Marriage can obscure sexual assault, since spouses cannot be forced to testify against each other even about events that took place before they married. It also deprives a minor of the right to have her parents support her, the protection of juvenile courts and departments of social services,[25] and the chance to apply for special immigrant juvenile status.[26]

EDUCATION

The state constitution guarantees a right to education[27] and promises equal opportunities for all students in the public schools.[28] By statute, every parent or "other person having charge or control of a child between the ages of seven and sixteen" must send the child to school.[29] A parent may be prosecuted for failing to do so.[30] In addition, failing to send a child to school can be considered neglect.[31]

24. Matthew Bramlett and William D. Mosher, "First Marriage Dissolution, Divorce and Remarriage: United States," *Advance Data,* No. 323, Centers for Disease Control and Prevention, National Center for Health Statistics (May 31, 2001). Available at http://www.cdc.gov/nchs/.

25. G.S. 7B-101(14).

26. Special immigrant status lets an undocumented minor who is declared dependent by a court in the United States remain in the country lawfully and eventually become a citizen. 8 U.S.C. § 1101(a)(27)(J).

27. N.C. Const. art. I, § 15; Leandro v. State, 346 N.C. 336, 488 S.E.2d 249 (1997); Sneed v. Greensboro City Bd. of Educ., 299 N.C. 609, 264 S.E.2d 106 (1980).

28. N.C. Const. art. IX, § 2.

29. G.S. 115C-378.

30. G.S. 115C-380.

31. *In re* McMillan, 30 N.C. App. 235, 226 S.E.2d 693 (1976); *In re* Devone, 86 N.C. App. 57, 356 S.E.2d 389 (1987).

HEALTH CARE

Since parents must procure necessary medical care for their children,[32] parents usually have the legal right to control the care—arranging for it, consenting to it, and paying for it. Another reason why parents consent to treatment for minors is that minors cannot enter into binding contracts. Therefore health providers may not be paid for services if the minor alone consented to them.

In a few states the law considers older minors generally capable of making their own medical decisions, but North Carolina law does not. Still, in recent decades the General Assembly has made exceptions to the traditional rule that parents control the medical treatment of minors by identifying particular situations in which a minor may consent for herself, an adult other than the parent may consent for her, or a physician may treat her without consent.

Health care provided in schools is discussed later in the guide.

For legal information about minors' rights to information about pregnancy options, as well as rights respecting abortion, childbirth, parenting, contraception, sterilization, and treatment of sexually transmitted diseases, see Anne Dellinger and Arlene M. Davis, *Health Care for Pregnant Adolescents: A Legal Guide* (Chapel Hill, N.C.: Institute of Government, 2001), or Anne Dellinger, *Social Services for Pregnant and Parenting Adolescents: A Legal Guide* (Chapel Hill, N.C.: Institute of Government, 2002). Available at http://www.adolescentpregnancy.unc.edu.

PLACING A CHILD FOR ADOPTION OR
SURRENDERING A NEWBORN

A minor mother—not her parents or guardian—can place a child for adoption. The father—minor or adult, married or unmarried—can consent to the adoption or take steps to prevent it. Increasingly, biological parents can learn about or interact with potential adoptive parents before placing a child

32. G.S. 7B-101(15).

with them. Parents who relinquish a child and children relinquished for adoption are likely to be able to contact one another when the child has reached adulthood, if not before. **For more information on adoption, see Anne Dellinger and Arlene M. Davis, *Health Care for Pregnant Adolescents: A Legal Guide* (Chapel Hill, N.C.: Institute of Government, 2001), or Anne Dellinger, *Social Services for Pregnant and Parenting Adolescents: A Legal Guide* (Chapel Hill, N.C.: Institute of Government, 2002). Available at http://www.adolescentpregnancy.unc.edu.**

A state law enacted in 2001 allows a parent to surrender a newborn. The law was in part a response to an incident in which a fourteen-year-old gave birth at school and abandoned the infant.[33] Expressing particular concern for children born to young parents,[34] the General Assembly set conditions to allow a parent to avoid criminal liability for abandonment when surrendering custody of an infant fewer than seven days old. If a parent offers a child to an adult and "does not express an intent to return," DSS workers, health care providers, emergency medical service workers, and law enforcement officers who are on duty or at their workplace *must*, and other adults *may*, accept the child.[35] The adult who takes the newborn must guard his or her health and well-being and immediately contact DSS or law enforcement. The person accepting a newborn may ask the parent's identity and medical history but must tell parents they are not required to answer. Any adult acting in good faith who accepts an infant is safe from civil or criminal liability unless she or he exhibits gross negligence, wanton misconduct, or intentional wrongdoing.[36]

For the parent, surrendering a newborn in compliance with the statute

33. Lea Delicio, *Schools, officials try to reach out to pregnant teens: Birth in bathroom at middle school proves need exists,* THE TIMES NEWS (Burlington, N.C.), Feb. 22, 2000.

34. S.L. 2001-291, Section 6.

35. G.S. 7B-500(b) and (d).

36. The immunity does not extend to "gross negligence, wanton conduct, or intentional wrongdoing." G.S. 7B-500(e).

protects against a charge of abandonment[37] or the milder forms of child abuse.[38] However, if a parent abandons a newborn for sixty consecutive days, and a petition to terminate parental rights is filed at the end of that period, the court has grounds for termination.[39]

EMPLOYMENT

Although teen mothers are often eager to work,[40] the current thrust of U.S. law and policy is that schooling is more important for minors. To qualify for several kinds of federal–state assistance a pregnant or parenting minor must attend school, and a teen head-of-household meets the work requirement for receiving assistance as long as she is in school.[41] But, the same programs require work of most custodial parents who are not in school[42] and of the non-custodial parent of a minor's child. More than half a million mothers in the United States under age twenty work. The large majority are unmarried and, of that group, nearly 52 percent work or are actively looking for work.[43]

37. G.S. 14-322.3.

38. G.S. 14-318.2. For a parent convicted of felony child abuse under G.S. 14-318.4, abandonment in compliance with this statute may be considered a mitigating factor in sentencing.

39. G.S. 7B-1111(a)(7). For who may file a petition, see G.S. 7B-1103.

40. JUDITH MUSICK, YOUNG, POOR, AND PREGNANT: THE PSYCHOLOGY OF TEENAGE MOTHERHOOD 197 (1993).

41. 42 U.S.C. § 607(c)(2)(C) (Supp. 2001).

42. North Carolina Department of Health and Human Services, Division of Social Services, North Carolina Temporary Assistance for Needy Families State Plan, FFY 2002–2003, Raleigh (2001), at 22. Available at http://www.dhhs.state.nc.us/dss/docs/stateplan.pdf. The custodial parent of a child fewer than twelve months old is exempt (if she has not used this exemption before), as is a parent who cannot find care for a child under six years old.

43. In March 2002 there were 405,000 sixteen- to nineteen-year-old mothers; 296,000 unmarried, 109,000 married. Of the unmarried group, 161,000 were in the labor force, defined as employed or seeking employment; 129,000 were employed. Information provided by Howard Hayghe, (202) 691-6380, an economist at the U.S. Bureau of Labor Statistics, May 29, 2003.

Although no count of North Carolina's employed minor parents is available, certainly many have jobs.

North Carolina's youth employment statute[44] and regulations[45] penalize almost anyone who hires a minor without a work permit. These laws incorporate the child labor provisions of the federal Fair Labor Standards Act[46] and its regulations[47] and contain other provisions as well. Under state law it is usually local DSS directors who issue work permits to minors living or planning to work in the county.[48]

In general, these are the legal conditions for youth employment. No one thirteen or younger may work. Fourteen- and fifteen-year-olds may work only in certain occupations and outside school hours. Sixteen- and seventeen-year-olds may work somewhat longer hours with written permission from a parent and a school official; however, their jobs may not be hazardous or harmful to their health or well-being. Emancipated minors, like all other minors, must comply with the conditions.[49] If the minor is married the state Department of Labor has the minor's spouse—instead of parent or guardian —sign the permit.[50] The application for a youth employment certificate (job permit) can be printed from http://www.nclabor.com.

44. G.S. 95-25.5.

45. 13 NCAC 12.0401 through 12.0406; 12.0501; 12.0701 and 12.0702.

46. 29 U.S.C. § 212.

47. 29 C.F.R. § 570.117, *et seq.*

48. DSS directors and the Commissioner of Labor share responsibility. Subject to the Labor Department's approval, a director may delegate responsibility. G.S. 95-25.5(a). Some DSS directors have delegated, usually to local school officials or, less often, to public libraries' staff. Telephone conversation with Shannon Council, Youth Employment Specialist, North Carolina Department of Labor, June 8, 2001.

49. Communication from Henry D. Sasser, Deputy Administrator, Wage and Hour Bureau, N.C. Department of Labor, June 24, 2003.

50. N.C. Department of Labor, *A Guide to Youth Employment Laws and Regulations for Issuing Youth Employment Certificates.* Telephone conversation with Barbara Jackson, attorney for the North Carolina Department of Labor, June 15, 2001. This policy is curently under review.

Schools' Responsibility for Pregnant and Parenting Students

HOW THESE STUDENTS FARE IN SCHOOL

Twenty years ago the National Institute of Education reported, "Local education agency (LEA) responses to student pregnancy and parenthood are constrained by a number of factors, including narrow (usually medical) definitions of the problem; opposition to sex education, contraception and abortion; disagreement about the appropriate school role; lack of expertise; and a lack of incentives to develop programs."[1] Despite some improvement —a modest amount of federal funding for adolescent parenting programs, for example—these problems still exist.

Fortunately, some pregnant and parenting students meet school counselors, social workers, nurses, teachers, or administrators who expect them to continue their education and who help to make it possible. Many such dedicated people work in North Carolina's schools. The speaker below is a school social worker:

> My work is supposed to be with kids who've had court involvement, but I take the pregnant girls as extras because they're not being served. We had twenty this year. One is thirteen and too sick to stay in school any longer. She's thirteen or fourteen weeks pregnant and probably won't be back in school till the baby's born. A DSS report has been made about her. Our DSS takes any report of this kind these days because in the past they wouldn't and things turned out badly.[2]

1. Gail L. Zellman, *The Response of the Schools to Teenage Pregnancy and Parenthood (*Rand Corporation, April 1981), quotation at v (hereafter Rand Corporation Report).

2. Author's interview, Adolescent Pregnancy Prevention Coalition of North Carolina (APPCNC) Annual Conference, Greensboro, North Carolina, May 4, 2000.

A high school graduate, former foster child, and nineteen-year-old mother of three paid tribute to educators like the one above. Asked whether she had considered dropping out, she exclaimed, "My teachers would never have let me do that! They'd have come and gotten me."[3]

Other students are less fortunate. The youngest girls are in a particularly difficult position, especially with peers.[4] Occasionally, school personnel seem to single a girl out as a disgraceful example. National Honor Society chapters have barred or expelled pregnant or parenting girls on the basis of character.[5] (Litigation on this point is described in the following section.) In North Carolina, a homecoming queen who was disqualified alleged that her unmarried motherhood was the reason.[6] North Carolina social workers, physicians with teen patients, and school and health department nurses told the author about these incidents:

- One student, angry about another's pregnancy, threatens her in phone calls and pushes her at school. When the pregnant girl's parents, who have tapes of the calls, contact the school they are told that the school can only offer homebound instruction.

- Near the beginning of a student's pregnancy her doctor orders bed rest. The principal says no teacher is—or will be— available for homebound instruction.

3. Author's interview, Durham, N.C., February 15, 2001.

4. "Junior high school students we interviewed told us many students were hostile, and good friends often deserted. One who had become pregnant at thirteen said she was often called a 'whore' and was involved in many fights. 'Being pregnant in high school is easier,' she said." Rand Corporation Report at 90.

5. Members must display scholarship (B or higher average), service, leadership, and character. The last requires upholding "principles of morality and ethics" and maintaining "a good and clean lifestyle." *See* "Membership," at http://www.nhs.us/membership.

6. *Homecoming queen finds role in dispute*, THE NEWS & OBSERVER (Raleigh, N.C.), October 14, 1999, 3A, Cols. 2–4.

- Pregnant students could get optimal care at a hospital teen clinic in an adjoining county. Because the school requires makeup time for medical appointments, most refuse the opportunity as it would frequently extend the school day to five p.m.

- A girl who gave birth in early August asks to return to school September 1. Another, with a Thanksgiving due date, who plans to breast-feed, asks to return after Christmas. Both requests are denied under a policy stating that no student receives semester credit if more than ten days are missed.

- A pregnant girl's mother orders her to leave home in New York and the girl comes to North Carolina where her father lives. He sometimes lets her sleep at his house but won't miss work to enroll her in school. The school will not accept her without his registering her, nor let him come to sign the forms before or after his workday.

In interviews, so many school employees mentioned a greater burden for middle-school students that the issue merits separate attention. Informants' comments on this subject are summarized below.[7]

- School nurse: Middle school administrators are really uptight about what they refer to as the "p" word. They're very eager to get pregnant girls [out of school and] on homebound [instruction].

- Central office administrator: A middle school student who gives birth and keeps her child is likely to find it hard fitting in with her peers thereafter. She is usually not as well accepted as an older girl, which makes it harder for her to remain in school.

7. While the author's interview notes contain direct quotations, they also summarize what speakers conveyed.

- Three middle school guidance counselors, interviewed together: It's much harder to be pregnant or parenting here than high school. Anyone different sticks out at this age. The girls in this situation may already have been retained. Often they have very little in common with classmates. They're here mainly because of the [compulsory attendance] law. Sometimes I'm just praying a girl can make it till she gets to high school. The biggest educational barrier for these students is having to combine school, work, and taking care of a child. Child care is a major problem. These kids come late and tired. They can't do the same homework other kids can. They often miss whole days for child care. I feel for them here [in middle school]—they don't fit in any more. They have adult responsibilities and they're sitting next to children. I have one girl now, a special education student, and it's sad to see how the emotional stress and embarrassment of being pregnant are negatively affecting her learning.

- A supervisor of school nurses: A parenting student's return is much harder for a middle school to accept. The school doesn't want them, though you'll never get them to admit this. Staff fears the influence on other kids: they are uncomfortable when the new mother even visits. A second problem for staff is simply knowing how to treat the girl.

- The same supervisor of school nurses: Another deterrent to finishing school is subsequent pregnancy. In my experience the youngest mothers are highly likely to have another pregnancy soon. I just don't remember any thirteen-year-old, say, who didn't have another child until she was twenty. (This woman pointed out how many programs for teen parents will not accept anyone with more than one child.)

Teens also complain about their school experiences when pregnant or parenting—about being removed from the normal school program during pregnancy; barred from field trips, physical education, sports, or R.O.T.C.; and simply treated differently ("as if your life is over because of having a child.")[8] For insight into the experiences and emotions of girls in such situations, see Wendy Luttrell's *Pregnant Bodies, Fertile Minds: Gender, Race, and The Schooling of Pregnant Teens.*[9] For five years Luttrell studied participants in a school-based parenting program in "a mid-sized industrial city in the Piedmont region of North Carolina."

There is other evidence of barriers for these students. In 2000 the Reproductive Rights Project of the New York Civil Liberties Union asked to meet with New York City's Education Chancellor about "numerous complaints of pregnant students who are 'eased out,' 'counseled out,' or simply pushed out of school."[10] In an effort to confirm the complaints, the project had its interns call schools and pose as pregnant students who wanted to enroll in regular high school programs. In talking with twenty-eight staff members at twelve high schools they found that "three schools refused to even consider enrolling pregnant students in good academic standing, while eight others actively discouraged them,"[11] and that "responses varied greatly even in an individual

8. ACLU-NC survey answered by eighty-one public school students in Adolescent Parenting programs, October 1999 to January 2000.

9. WENDY LUTTRELL, PREGNANT BODIES, FERTILE MINDS: GENDER, RACE, AND THE SCHOOLING OF PREGNANT TEENS (New York, Routledge 2003).

10. New York Civil Liberties Union, *Letter to NYC Education Chancellor Levy Concerning High School Admissions Practices Regarding Pregnant and Parenting Teens* (August 3, 2000), available at http://nyclu.org/rrp_chancellor1.html. The Civil Liberties Union rejected a counter offer to meet with administrators of alternative education programs. *Follow-up Letter to NYC Education Chancellor Levy Concerning High School Admissions Practices Regarding Pregnant and Parenting Teens* (December 1, 2000), available at http://nyclu.org/rrp_chancellor2.html. *See also* Jennifer Medina and Tamar Lewin, *High School Under Scrutiny for Giving Up on Its Students*, NEW YORK TIMES, August 1, 2003.

11. New York Civil Liberties Union, *Survey of New York City High School Admissions Practices Regarding Pregnant and Parenting Teens* (December 1, 2000), available at http://www.nyclu.org/rrp_p_survey.html, at 3.

school, depending on who answered the phone."[12] For more information on how pregnant and parenting students fare in North Carolina schools, see "Improving School Policies," below.

PROTECTION AGAINST DISCRIMINATION

The United States and State Constitutions

In the United States in the second half of the twentieth century, the social stigma attached to early and especially to unmarried childbearing diminished. The social change was more strongly reflected in statutory and regulatory law than in case law. There are no binding court decisions holding that the United States or North Carolina constitutions protect the education rights of pregnant or parenting minors. Still, one can reasonably assume that both constitutions offer some protection.

Not long ago the United States Supreme Court reaffirmed that the U.S. Constitution forbids gender discrimination, in a case forbidding a state to maintain a single-sex university.[13] Thus far, the U.S. Supreme Court has not seen pregnancy discrimination as gender discrimination,[14] but a few lower federal courts have held that it is discriminatory for schools to discipline pregnant girls but not boys who father a child. [See "Extracurricular activities (National Honor Society)," below.]

Also, while there are no decisions binding in North Carolina, it is reasonable to think that schools would violate the U.S. Constitution by penalizing students for bearing and raising children. Government, including public schools, must have a rational basis for rules that burden individuals. At a minimum, rules must be arguably likely to produce the intended results. Otherwise, a rule violates the Fourteenth Amendment guarantees of no deprivation of life, liberty, or property without due process of law and no denial of the equal protection of the laws to any person within the nation's jurisdiction. Even before 1930, the first state courts had struck down school disciplinary

12. *Id.* at 1.
13. United States v. Virginia, 518 U.S. 515 (1996).
14. Geduldig v. Aiello, 417 U.S. 484 (1974).

measures against married students and parents as arbitrary and capricious,[15] and the trend strengthened in the decades preceding Title IX.[16] Since 1972, when Title IX was enacted, such discriminatory rules have rarely been adopted.

North Carolina courts do not seem to have ruled on gender discrimination in public education. However, our state constitution and our state supreme court's interpretation of constitutional requirements for education[17] emphasize commitment to *all* North Carolinians: "The people have a right to the privilege of education, and it is the duty of the State to guard and maintain that right."[18] The state constitution instructs the General Assembly to create public schools "wherein equal opportunities shall be provided for all students."[19] The North Carolina Supreme Court has found that the state constitution guarantees "every child of this state an opportunity to receive a sound basic education in our public schools,"[20] and the court interprets "sound basic education" quite broadly.[21] Thus, it is likely that denying an education on the basis of pregnancy or parental status would violate North Carolina's constitution.

15. Nutt v. Bd. of Education, 128 Kan. 507, 278 P. 1065 (1929); McLeod v. State *ex rel.* Colmer, 154 Miss. 468, 122 So. 737 (1929).

16. Brian E. Berwick and Carol Oppenheimer, *Marriage, Pregnancy, and the Right to Go to School,* 50 Tex. L. Rev. 1196, 1197–1211 (1972) (hereafter Berwick and Oppenheimer).

17. Leandro v. State of North Carolina, 346 N.C. 336 (1997). *See also* Ann McColl, Leandro: *Constitutional Adequacy in Education and Standards-Based Reforms,* 32 School Law Bulletin 1 (Chapel Hill, N.C., Institute of Government, Summer 2001) and John Charles Boger, Leandro v. State—*A New Era in Educational Reform?* 29 School Law Bulletin 9 (Chapel Hill, N.C., Institute of Government, Summer 1998).

18. N.C. Const. art. I, § 15.

19. N.C. Const. art. IX, § 2(1), *id.*

20. Leandro v. State of North Carolina, 346 N.C. 336 at 347.

21. "For purposes of our [North Carolina] Constitution, a 'sound basic education' is one that will provide the student with at least: (1) sufficient ability to read, write, and speak the English language and a sufficient knowledge of fundamental mathematics and physical science to enable the student to function in a complex and rapidly changing society; (2) sufficient fundamental knowledge of geography, history, and basic economic and political systems to enable the student to make informed choices with regard to issues that affect the student personally or affect the

Title IX and Related Legislation

The legal status of pregnant and parenting students changed significantly in 1972 when Congress forbade any education program that receives federal funds from discriminating on the basis of sex.[22] "Title IX," as the law is called, applies to every public school system in the United States, as well as to almost all colleges. Title IX abruptly altered the accepted social and educational norms for girls and women. Twenty-five years after its passage, the U.S. Secretary of Education said, "America is a more equal, more educated and more prosperous nation because of the far-reaching effects of this legislation."[23] This section describes the status of pregnant and parenting students before Title IX; the act and its regulations; litigation over Title IX in public schools; and ways in which the U.S. Department of Education enforces the law.

Federal statutes enacted after Title IX amplified its effect. The Women's Educational Equity Act (1974) funded materials on gender equality in schools, authorized model projects, and awarded challenge grants for innovation. Its 2001 reauthorization finds that "pregnant and parenting teenagers are at high risk for dropping out of school and existing dropout prevention programs do not adequately address the needs of such teenagers."[24] Among other provisions, the act authorizes technical support for schools to help "pregnant students and students rearing children to remain in or to return to secondary school, graduate, and prepare their preschool children to start

---

student's community, state, and nation; (3) sufficient academic and vocational skills to enable the student to successfully engage in postsecondary education or vocational training; and (4) sufficient academic and vocational skills to enable the student to compete on an equal basis with others in further formal education or gainful employment in contemporary society." *Id.*

22. 20 U.S.C. § 1681. Title IX's regulations are at 34 C.F.R. Part 106. Guidelines on eliminating gender discrimination in vocational education are at 45 C.F.R. Part 80, Appendix B.

23. Richard W. Riley, *Title IX: 25 Years of Progress,* U.S. Department of Education (June 1997), available at http://www.ed.gov/pubs/TitleIX/title.html.

24. 20 U.S.C. § 7283.

school."[25] Schools may also seek federal assistance to help with the cost of Title IX compliance.[26] Statutes on gender equity in vocational education are discussed below under "Vocational Education."

Before Title IX

In the first three-quarters of the twentieth century, pregnancy almost always suspended a girl's schooling and raising a child brought a permanent end to elementary or secondary education. Despite a few advocates of change, most school boards were unwilling to enroll these young women or even provide instruction in maternity homes. Rickie Solinger, in *Wake Up Little Susie: Single Pregnancy and Race before* Roe v. Wade, describes the era and notes a growing willingness in the late 1950s and early 1960s to begin "eradicating the contradiction between the statuses of 'unwed mother' and 'student.'"[27]

In North Carolina a 1964 letter from the Deputy Attorney General conveys views typical of the period—though more sympathetic to the student than usual. The Deputy Attorney General wrote to a school attorney who asked whether "the mother of [an] illegitimate child should return to school:"[28]

> We have been called upon to write many letters in regard to this situation relating to the birth of an illegitimate child where one of the pupils is the mother. The reasonable and sound judgment of the school board in enacting a rule in this regard would not be disturbed by the courts. We find from writing to school administrators and talking over the problem with them that the usual course is to suspend for a while and then let the student return if she shows any signs at all of regaining her character and re-establishing herself as a reasonably proper person.

25. 20 U.S.C. § 7283b(b)(2).

26. *Id.*

27. RICKIE SOLINGER, WAKE UP LITTLE SUSIE: SINGLE PREGNANCY AND RACE BEFORE ROE V. WADE at 129–130 (New York and London, Routledge 1992).

28. Letter of Ralph Moody to Koy E. Dawkins, October 17, 1964, *North Carolina Attorney General Rulings: Schools and Education 1964–66*, VI, F.

Of course, if such a pupil after returning to school engages in further immoral or disreputable conduct or proves to be a menace to the school, then such person can be permanently dismissed.

It is a rather serious matter in a world of our kind which accents skills and education to deprive a person of an education. We suggest the person in question be allowed to return to school on probation and then the school administrators can observe the reaction and see how the matter works out. If it should turn out that because of this situation too many problems are created, then a permanent dismissal would be in order but a trial should be made of the pupil returning to school. It is simply too great a human responsibility to sit in judgment and condemn a person entirely or permanently from an educational standpoint for one misstep.

Although a few courts recognized a limited right for pregnant students to attend school in the late 1960s and early 1970s,[29] only Title IX effected far-reaching change.[30]

29. *E.g.*, Perry v. Grenada Munic. Sch. Dist., 300 F. Supp. 748 (N.D. Miss. 1969) (unwed mothers entitled to readmission unless "their presence in school would taint the education of other students"); Houston v. Prosser, 361 F. Supp. 295 (N.D. Ga. 1973) (school could require fifteen-year-old mother to attend at night, but not to pay tuition and buy books). See also Ordway v. Hargraves, 323 F. Supp. 1155 (D. Mass. 1971), simply ordering readmission. For a review of the law at the time, see Berwick and Oppenheimer, note 16 above.

30. How far-reaching is debatable. A researcher who studied a North Carolina LEA's program for pregnant students over five years concluded that "Title IX may have ended de jure discrimination but it did not end de facto discrimination against pregnant schoolgirls." WENDY LUTRELL, Chapter One, *Separate and Unequal*, in PREGNANT BODIES, FERTILE MINDS: GENDER, RACE, AND THE SCHOOLING OF PREGNANT TEENS 20–21 (New York, Routledge 2003).

Rights to Stay in School and Be Treated Equally

Title IX regulations require the following with respect to pregnancy and related conditions:[31]

- Schools cannot discriminate against pregnant students or exclude them from school, or any program, class or extra-curricular activity.[32]

- Enrollment in an alternative program or school must be completely voluntary.[33]

- An alternative program must be comparable in quality and academic offerings to the regular curriculum.[34]

- Schools can require a doctor's certification that a pregnant girl is physically and emotionally able to participate in school or a particular school activity only if certification is required of all students under a doctor's care.[35]

- Excused absences for pregnancy and related conditions must be granted for the length of time the student's doctor finds medically necessary.[36]

31. "Related conditions" include childbirth, false pregnancy, termination of pregnancy and recovery from any of these conditions, 34 C.F.R. § 106.40(b).

32. 34 C.F.R. § 106.31.

33. *Id.* While alternative programs can offer valuable support, there is a widespread perception that they are not academically comparable to the regular curriculum. *See, e.g.,* Monica J. Stamm, *"A Skeleton in the Closet," Single-Sex Schools for Pregnant Girls,* 98 COLUM. L. REV. 1203–1237 (1998). In this regard it is interesting that G.S. 115C-47(32a) "urges local boards to adopt policies that prohibit superintendents from assigning to any alternative learning program any professional public school employee who has received within the last three years a rating on a formal evaluation that is less than above standard."

Stamm also questions whether an alternative program is "voluntary" if it is much more accommodating of pregnant students' needs than the LEAs' regular programs. In other words, has a school created an alternative program to avoid keeping pregnant students in the regular program? *Id.* at note 188 (citation omitted).

34. 34 C.F.R. § 106.40(b)(3).

35. 34 C.F.R. § 106.40(b)(2).

36. 34 C.F.R. § 106.40(b)(5).

- After a medically necessary absence a student must be restored to the academic and extracurricular status she held when the leave began.[37]
- A health service or insurance coverage offered to other students with temporary disabilities must be offered to these students.[38]

Every school district must designate a Title IX coordinator, to whom students or parents may complain, and publish his or her name and address. The district must also establish and publicize a grievance process.[39]

Title IX has less to say about parenting than pregnancy. However, it does establish an important principle for schools' treatment of parents—equality on the basis of sex. The regulations forbid schools to, on the basis of sex, "Subject any person to separate or different rules of behavior, sanctions, or other treatment."[40] Another provision prohibits schools from applying "any rule concerning a student's actual or potential parental, family, or marital status which treats students differently on the basis of sex."[41] Nearly all custodial parents in school are female. Therefore, the effect of the principle is largely to protect young mothers from discrimination, but a father too could invoke Title IX—for example, to place his child in the school's daycare facilities or to enroll in a parenting class.

Title IX only requires schools to treat male and female students alike and not to discriminate against pregnant students. However, as noted earlier (see "The United States and State Constitutions," above), constitutional principles would likely prevent a school from penalizing married students or parents of both sexes or custodial parents.

37. *Id.*
38. 34 C.F.R. § 106.40(b)(4).
39. 34 C.F.R. § 106.8.
40. 34 C.F.R. § 106.31(b)(4).
41. 34 C.F.R. § 106.40(a).

Extracurricular Activities (National Honor Society)

Before Title IX[42] (and in some cases after it) schools tried penalties short of exclusion—such as barring students from extracurricular activities—to discourage sex, marriage, and parenting. Students seem to have cared most—aside from sports—about exclusion from the National Honor Society (NHS). Several girls who were kept from joining or who were dismissed from the society tested Title IX's equality principle.[43] Their cases, described below, show that courts will enforce the regulation that pregnant or parenting students may participate in *any* school activity if they are physically able and otherwise qualified.

The National Association of Secondary School Principals (NASSP), which sponsors the NHS and a similar organization for middle schools, estimates that local chapters enroll more than a million students.[44] They and their families are said to value membership for the society's activities; as the school's recognition of the student's excellence; and as an honor that may help with college admission, financial aid, and employment.[45] Conversely, when a student meets the academic criterion, *not* being selected for NHS can be seen as posing a question about her integrity. Dismissal is viewed as even more damaging.[46]

The NHS describes itself as "more than just an honor roll."[47] Selection is based on scholarship, service, leadership, and character. A person of character

---

42. *See, e.g.,* Romans v. Crenshaw, 354 F. Supp. 868 (S.D. Texas 1972) (ban on extracurriculars for divorced student violates equal protection clause of U.S. Constitution) and Warren v. National Association of Secondary School Principals, 375 F. Supp. 1043 (N.D. Texas 1974) (expulsion from Honor Society without due process violates student's liberty interest in reputation).

43. For a general review, see Thomas A. Schweitzer, *"A" Students Go to Court: Is Membership in the National Honor Society a Cognizable Legal Right?* 50 Syracuse L. Rev. 63–107 (2000).

44. See "About Us" on the NHS Web site, http://www.nhs.us.

45. Romans v. Crenshaw, 354 F. Supp. 868, at 869.

46. Warren v. National Association of Secondary School Principals, 375 F. Supp. 1043, at 1048 (N.D. Texas 1974).

47. "About Us," http://www.nhs.us.

"upholds principles of morality and ethics, is cooperative, demonstrates high standards of honesty and reliability, shows courtesy, concern, and respect for others and generally maintains a good and clean lifestyle."[48] The national office of the NHS acknowledges that Title IX forbids excluding students on the basis of pregnancy but tells chapters that "the sexual behavior of a student can be properly considered as an aspect of character . . . and pregnancy is a legitimate evidential fact which can be considered in evaluating such behavior."[49] However, the office advises, "[P]regnancy can be so considered only if evidence of paternity is similarly regarded as indicative of character."[50]

The national office of the NHS also suggests why its chapters might not want to discriminate against pregnant students or young mothers.[51] First, by meeting the society's academic and service requirements pregnant and parenting students have beaten the odds and their "personal responsibility and initiative . . . should be rewarded whenever possible." Second, these students, more than others, need the school's and their peers' support. Third, a chapter may not be able to prove that it applies a no-premarital-sex standard fairly. The national office advises chapters to consult the school attorney before acting and, whatever the outcome, to pay such students "special attention in order to guarantee both the successful completion of the mother's schooling, but also the strong development of the new child."

Occasionally, news stories appear about teen mothers or pregnant students who were denied school honors,[52] and college students are challenging

48. "Membership," *Id.*

49. *NHS National Handbook,* Appendix 7, at 90 (1997 Edition). The Handbook is currently being revised.

50. *Id.*

51. "Additional considerations beyond formal policy statements" (internal memorandum dated 2/25/97, in the author's files).

52. Stephanie Sandoval, *Cheerleader faces criticism while juggling motherhood, high school,* THE DALLAS MORNING NEWS, June 12, 2000, at 4A; Dan Jewel and Barbara Sandler, *A Question of Honor: Barred from her school's honor society, an unwed teenage mother fights back,* PEOPLE, June 15, 1998, at 149.

the denial of athletic opportunities.[53] So far, however, all of the reported cases concerning extracurricular activities in secondary education involve the NHS. Three of the decisions, described below, are based on Title IX; the other, on constitutional grounds.

In 1982 Loretta Wort was dismissed from the NHS—she claimed, for pregnancy; the school claimed, for premarital sex. A federal district court ruled that her dismissal violated Title IX and the Fourteenth Amendment to the U.S. Constitution. The court ordered the school's NHS chapter to reinstate her and awarded Wort costs and attorney fees of over $20,000.[54]

On similar facts Arlene Pfeiffer accused her school of violating Title IX and the Pennsylvania Equal Rights Amendment when it dismissed her from the society in 1983. The school won at trial, with the court finding that the dismissal was for premarital sex, not pregnancy.[55] The court of appeals did not label that conclusion clearly erroneous. However, it sent the case back, telling the judge to hear one of Ms. Pfeiffer's witnesses who had wanted to testify that he fathered a child and was not dismissed from the society. The appellate judges said, "We believe that [his] evidence has the potential of being relevant to whether the council members followed a double standard in evaluating premarital sexual activities of NHS members. Under these circumstances, to exclude it was not consistent with sound exercise of discretion."[56] If the lower court, after hearing his testimony, were to conclude that the school's reason was a pretext, Pfeiffer could be awarded damages under the state and federal statutes.[57]

---

53. In March 2003, Tara Brady, a Division I basketball player, filed an action in U.S. District Court against Sacred Heart University claiming discrimination on the basis of pregnancy and parenting. Thomas B. Scheffey, *Pregnant Athlete Seeks Title IX Change*, THE CONNECTICUT LAW TRIBUNE, April 7, 2003, at http://www.law.com.

54. The district court order was not reported. The court of appeals later dismissed as untimely the school district's appeal of the costs and fees award. Wort v. Vierling, 778 F.2d. 1233 (7th Cir. 1985).

55. Pfeiffer v. Marion Center Areas Sch. Dist., 700 F. Supp. 269 (W.D. Pa. 1988).

56. Pfeiffer v. Marion Center Area Sch. Dist., 917 F.2d 779 (3d. Cir. 1990), at 786.

57. *Id.* at 788. On rehearing, the lower court again held for the school.

In the early 1990s Elisa Cazares was denied admission to the NHS because, according to a federal district court,[58] she was pregnant, unmarried, and not living with the father of her child. When the court ordered the school not to hold an NHS induction ceremony without her the school cancelled the ceremony. The court then awarded Cazares attorney fees higher than the statutory cap and a majority of the 9th Circuit Court of Appeals affirmed the award.[59] (Title IX does not seem to have been an issue in the case.)[60]

In 1998 three unmarried mothers were denied admission to the society—Amanda Lemon of Xenia, Ohio,[61] who did not sue, and Somer Chipman and Chasity Glass of Covington, Kentucky, who did. Ms. Chipman and Glass, who had 3.9 and 3.7 averages respectively, were the only ones among thirty-three students with 3.5 or higher averages not chosen for the NHS.[62] The court ordered the school district to admit the girls, saying this about the premarital sex versus pregnancy dispute:

> There is strong evidence that the . . . selection committee considered the fact that each plaintiff had engaged in premarital sexual activity and had given birth to a child out of wedlock. There is further strong evidence that the selection committee did not ask those students offered admission to the NHS—male or female—if they had engaged in premarital sexual activity. [Court's footnote: "The court certainly does not suggest they should have done so."] However, the evidence before the court indicates that the committee would have considered any

58. The opinion is not reported. These facts are stated in the appellate opinion, Cazares v. Barber, 959 F.2d 753 (9th Cir. 1992).

59. Id.

60. The dissent in the 9th Circuit indicates that the lower court decision rested on due process and equal protection grounds. Title IX is not mentioned in either the majority or dissenting opinion.

61. Dan Jewel and Barbara Sandler, A Question of Honor; Barred from her school's honor society, an unwed teenage mother fights back, PEOPLE, June 15, 1998.

62. Ethan Bronner, Lawsuit on Sex Bias by 2 Mothers, 17, NEW YORK TIMES, August 6, 1998, at A12, Cols. 4–6.

evidence of paternity in evaluating the character of male students, but that it was unlikely that any such knowledge would come before the committee in any way but rumor and gossip.[63]

Chipman may indicate what future courts will do because it is the most recent case and because it involves the most typical situation—school personnel willing, in theory, to treat young mothers and fathers alike, but in fact not doing so.

Vocational Education

All students, especially those who are supporting children, could benefit from work training. As a high school graduate who was a mother at fifteen put it, "After Ashley was born I realized that you can't raise a family on a high school diploma and a certificate from a cosmetology school." The young woman, formerly a low-performing student, was entering Morgan State University to study electrical engineering.[64]

As stated earlier, Title IX regulations require schools to let every student take advantage of the entire curriculum, including vocational education, and take part in all school activities.[65] Schools must also hold the parties they deal with, such as private companies offering work to vocational education students, to the same nondiscriminatory conduct.[66] The Vocational Education Act of 1963 was amended in 1976 to require states to eliminate sex discrimination, bias, and stereotyping in vocational education and to devote a specified portion of any federal funds awarded under the act to pregnant teens and single parents. The current federal vocational education act no longer reserves a

63. Chipman v. Grant County School District, 30 F. Supp. 2d 975, at 977 (E.D. Ky. 1998).

64. Jennifer Lee, *Rebirth of a Student: Mom, 18, Does Academic About-Face,* WASHINGTON POST, August 29, 1998, B1, Cols. 2–3.

65. "A recipient shall not provide any course or otherwise carry out any of its education program or activity separately on the basis of sex, or require or refuse participation therein by any of its students on such basis, including . . . industrial, business, vocational, technical . . . courses." 34 C.F.R. § 106.34.

66. 34 C.F.R. § 106.31(d).

particular portion of federal funds for these students. However, the act requires schools to assist "special populations," a term that includes single pregnant women and single parents.[67] States[68] and local agencies[69] must focus their efforts on the "special populations" and monitor their progress in vocational education and training programs.[70] Another federal statute, the Workforce Investment Act of 1998,[71] aims to improve job training for low-income youth, develop their leadership and other skills, and offer mentoring and employment opportunities.[72] Like the vocational education act, it names pregnant and parenting youth as appropriate candidates for special assistance.

North Carolina law, like the federal funding statutes, instructs the State Board of Education to make vocational and technical education "available to all students who desire it"[73] and not to approve any plans or funding applications for local programs that are inconsistent with that goal.[74] Another state statute allows the State Board of Education to accept federal funds for vocational and technical education.[75] The Department of Public Instruction (DPI) distributes the funds, based on a formula, to school districts and community colleges, each of which decides how to use its money.

Despite all these laws requiring gender equity, vocational classes in North Carolina public schools remain highly segregated by sex (as are the fields for which the programs prepare students). This is true throughout the United States, but especially in the South.[76] The National Women's Law Center (NWLC) blames schools for the segregation:

67. 20 U.S.C.A. § 2302(23).

68. 20 U.S.C.A. § 2342 and 2344.

69. 20 U.S.C.A. § 2354.

70. 20 U.S.C.A. § 2023(c)(2). Some LEAs have a special populations coordinator to assess students' needs. Telephone conversation with June Atkinson, North Carolina Department of Public Instruction, September 2, 2003.

71. 29 U.S.C.A. § 2801, *et seq.*

72. 29 U.S.C.A. § 2854. "Low-income" is defined in 29 U.S.C.A. § 2801(25).

73. G.S. 115C-151.

74. G.S. 115C-154.1(1).

75. G.S. 115C-155.

76. American Institutes for Research, *Gender Gaps: Where Schools Still Fail Our Children*, New York: American Association of University Women Educational Foundation (1999), at 123–124.

Biased counseling, the provision of incomplete information to students on the consequences of their career training choices, sexual harassment of girls who enroll in non-traditional classes, and other forms of discrimination conspire today to create a vocational system characterized by pervasive sex segregation. Young women remain clustered in 'traditionally female' programs that prepare them for low-wage careers. . . . Young men, on the other hand, fill the vast majority of slots in programs leading to higher-wage careers that can provide true economic self-sufficiency.[77]

In 2002 the NWLC reviewed female enrollment in technical and vocational programs,[78] asking every state for information and selecting twelve, including North Carolina, to study in detail. Using DPI's data, the NWLC reported that in North Carolina, cosmetology classes, for example, are 98 percent female; child care courses, 91 percent female; and health care training courses, 84 percent female. Other classes are very heavily male: electrical trades and welding courses are each 96 percent male; electronics, 95 percent male; masonry, automotive, and construction-related courses, 94 percent male; plumbing, 93 percent male; engineering-related courses, 93 percent male; and drafting, 87 percent male.[79]

NWLC also pointed out that the choices boys and girls are making will determine their wages. U.S. Department of Labor statistics, expressed in hourly wage ranges,[80] show the comparative economic rewards of certain male and female career paths:

77. National Women's Law Center, *Title IX and Equal Opportunity in Vocational and Technical Education: A Promise Still Owed to the Nation's Young Women,* Washington, D.C. (June 2002), available at http://www.nwlc.org, at 1.

78. *Id.* at 3.

79. *Petition for Compliance Review of High School Vocational and Technical Programs by the United States Department of Education, Office for Civil Rights, District of Columbia Office* (June 6, 2002), at 2 (hereafter *Petition for Compliance*).

80. The wage range compares the median hourly wage to that of the top 10 percent of workers in the field.

Cosmetology	$8.93/hr. to more than $15.97/hr.
Home health aide	$8.23/hr. to more than $11.93/hr.
Child care worker	$7.43/hr. to more than $10.71/hr.
Welding	$13.13/hr. to more than $23.32/hr.
Electrical and electronic installation and repair	$17.75/hr. to more than $25.78/hr.
Plumbing/pipefitting	$18.18/hr. to more than $30.06/hr.[81]

In 2002 the NWLC petitioned the U.S. Department of Education's Office for Civil Rights (OCR), asking it to investigate North Carolina's compliance with Title IX requirements on vocational education.[82] (NWLC filed a petition with respect to each of the twelve states in which it had reviewed compliance.) The petition noted North Carolina's failure to appoint a Title IX coordinator, as required by regulation,[83] and the very heavily male or female enrollment in many vocational education courses. NWLC claimed that the pattern "is likely caused and/or perpetuated by pervasive violations of Title IX and its implementing regulations and guidelines."

The Office for Civil Rights (OCR) agreed to investigate the failure to appoint a Title IX coordinator. (DPI has recently named one.) However, OCR refused to assume noncompliance "based on statistical data alone." In other words, OCR does not necessarily agree with the NWLC that schools are to blame for boys' and girls' choices in vocational education. OCR promised to continue to help insure that North Carolina LEAs comply with the federal vocational education guidelines,[84] especially as to career counseling materials, promotional and recruitment activities, and sexual harassment.[85]

81. *Petition for Compliance* 3.

82. *Id.*

83. 34 C.F.R. § 106.8.

84. Guidelines for Eliminating Discrimination and Denial of Services on the Basis of Race, Color, National Origin, Sex, and Handicap in Vocational Education Programs, 45 C.F.R. § Subtitle A (10-1-02 Edition) Pt. 80, App. B (hereafter Guidelines). Available at http://www.ed.gov/about/offices/list/ocr/docs/vocre/html.

85. Letter from Alice Wender to Marcia Greenberger, NWLC, January 21, 2003, copy in author's files.

Among other provisions, the federal vocational education guidelines require recipients[86] to

- tell students, parents, employees and the public annually that no one will be denied access to vocational education, training or work opportunities based on sex (or race, national origin, color, or handicap);[87]

- eliminate discrimination from counseling materials and activities and promotional and recruiting efforts;[88]

- see that counselors do not direct or urge students to sign up for a particular course or choose a career based on sex — or predict a student's success based on sex;[89]

- use both women and men, to the extent possible, as program recruiters and teachers;[90]

- refrain from promoting vocational education in a way that creates or perpetuates sex stereotypes (promotion includes actions of school officials, counselors, and vocational staff and activities such as career day, parents' night, and shop demonstrations, as well as the behavior of representatives of business and industry when visiting a school);[91]

- refrain from discriminating in awarding financial assistance;[92] and

86. Recipients may include boards and administrative agencies of these institutions: LEAs, vocational schools serving students from more than one district or people who have completed or left school, technical or community or four-year colleges, proprietary or private vocational schools. Guidelines I.C.
87. Guidelines IV.O.
88. Guidelines V.A.
89. Guidelines V.B.
90. Guidelines V.C.
91. Guidelines V.E.
92. Guidelines VI.B.

- refrain from allowing employers to discriminate in work-study, apprentice, or job placement programs to which students are referred.[93]

Equal Employment Opportunities for Girls

Title IX requires gender equality in vocational education in schools and community colleges. Other federal funding helps disadvantaged youth, in or out of school,[94] prepare for and enter the work force. The U.S. Department of Labor allocates funds to states for this purpose, and each state creates state and local "workforce investment boards" which award grants to program providers. School officials, along with business people, may sit on the local investment boards,[95] but elementary and secondary schools generally do not receive these funds.[96] Still, school staff can help pregnant and parenting students by telling them about the programs, which offer special opportunities to those groups.

The section of the federal act on youth activities funds programs for "improving educational and skill competencies," making "effective connections to employers," and supplying adult mentoring, and for supportive services (which can include transportation, child care and housing);[97] achievement incentives; and leadership opportunities."[98] To be eligible, a young woman or man must be between fourteen and twenty-one; low-income (as defined by statute);[99] and disadvantaged in one or more of the following ways:

93. Guidelines VII.

94. A substantial amount of a state's funds must be allocated to out-of-school youth, which can mean school dropouts or those who have a high school diploma or equivalent but still need assistance with employment. 29 U.S.C.A. § 2854(c)(4).

95. 29 U.S.C.A. § 2832.

96. Vocational education schools and nontraditional public schools may receive them, 29 U.S.C.A. § 2841(d)(3), but no funds can be used for services to students that would interfere with or replace regular academic requirements, 29 U.S.C.A. § 2854(c)(6)(C).

97. 29 U.S.C.A. § 2801(46).

98. 20 U.S.C.A. § 2854(a).

99. 29 U.S.C.A. § 2801(25).

- Deficient in basic literacy skills

- A school dropout

- Homeless, a runaway, or a foster child

- Pregnant or parenting

- A juvenile offender

- Someone who needs extra help to complete an educational program or get a job.[100]

(Up to 5 percent of program participants can fail to meet the income requirement, so long as they are in one of the six categories above.)[101] For youth aged sixteen to twenty-one, the Job Corps is a possibility and young parents are specifically targeted for it.[102]

Title IX Enforcement

The schools' record of voluntary compliance with Title IX seems mixed.[103] What are the possible consequences for violating the statute? In a school receiving federal funds, a student may sue the school system under Title IX,[104] asking for an injunction or damages.[105] The athletics provisions have been much litigated, including two cases involving pregnancy and athletics.[106]

---

100. 29 U.S.C.A. § 2801(13).

101. 29 U.S.C.A. § 2854(c)(5).

102. 29 U.S.C.A. § 2884.

103. A 1987 survey of schools in twelve districts nationwide by the Equity Center found Title IX violations in three-fourths of the schools sampled. *School Law News*, May 25, 1989, at 2. In 1995 Deborah Brake urged new efforts "to ensure that schools' treatment . . . complies with . . . Title IX." *Goals 2000 and Pregnant and Parenting Teens: Making Education Reform Attainable for Everyone*, Washington, D.C.: National Women's Law Center, at 8. See also text above at notes 8–10.

104. 42 U.S.C. § 2000d-7 (1994). Receipt of federal funds waives state immunity from suit under Title IX. 42 U.S.C. § 1687 (1994). An individual's right to sue was recognized in *Cannon v. University of Chicago*, 441 U.S. 677 (1979)

105. Franklin v. Gwinnett County Public Schools, 503 U.S. 60 (1992).

106. Gruenke v. Seip, 225 F.3d 290 (3d Cir. 2000) (coach violated high school swimmer's Fourth Amendment rights by requiring she take pregnancy test and due

Exclusion from the National Honor Society has provoked several cases (discussed above). The U.S. Supreme Court recognizes that schools violate Title IX by showing deliberate indifference to sexual harassment of students by other students.[107] Outside these areas, however, Title IX has produced little litigation. OCR investigations, rather than the courts, have been the primary means of enforcing the statute.

The Office for Civil Rights can investigate recipients of federal education funds on its own initiative or in response to a complaint. Unfortunately, school officials rarely have the chance to benefit from other districts' experience because it is hard to determine how often and with what results OCR conducts compliance reviews.[108] Certainly, at some points OCR has been concerned about violations of Title IX involving pregnancy and parenthood. In 1992 the OCR Director made a speech stating that 43 percent of girls who drop out do so because of pregnancy, parenting, or marriage; that boys or girls leaving for those reasons are less likely to return to school than others; and that the small number of complaints on these topics is not a reliable

---

process rights by failing to keep matter confidential). A Division I basketball player sued her former college and coach alleging that on revealing her pregnancy she was not "red shirted" as requested, lost her scholarship, and eventually transferred because the coach refused to speak to her. Grossman, Joanna, *A New Lawsuit by a Female Athlete Tests Title IX's Protection Against Pregnancy Discrimination,* available at http://writ.news.findlaw.com/grossman. Without admitting wrongdoing, the college settled for an undisclosed amount and "promised to clarify its existing policy prohibiting all discrimination on the basis of sex." Associated Press, *Athlete settles lawsuit against Sacred Heart University,* NEPA NEWS, October 21, 2003.

107. Davis v. Monroe County Bd. of Education, 526 U.S. 629 (1999).

108. In 1992 and 2001 the author made Freedom of Information Act requests for all Title IX compliance reviews OCR conducted after 1990 that involved student pregnancy or parenting. The 1992 request produced four reviews. The 2001 request yielded twenty—but the twenty did not include any of the first four. An OCR representative explained that the retrieval of only twenty-four documents resulted from OCR's recent conversion of some records to electronic form. Records that have not been converted remain in regional offices and are retrievable only on request to that office. Telephone conversation with Sandra P. Ward-Wooten, OCR, U.S. Department of Education, February 6, 2002.

indication of the extent of the problem. He also said that OCR's review of Atlanta's school system the previous year had found violations in treatment of these students; that six more reviews were in progress at that time; and that twenty-five more reviews on pregnancy/parenting were scheduled for the coming fiscal year.[109]

During the last decade OCR investigated complaints on these matters:

- Barring pregnant students from graduation[110]

- Student health policies that do not cover prenatal care and delivery[111]

- A pregnant student's removal from the list of orientation counselors, followed by a requirement that she submit a doctor's certificate that she was able to act as a counselor[112]

- Refusal to house students after the fourth month of pregnancy, in one case, and more than thirty days after a pregnancy diagnosis in another[113]

- Whether pregnant students were told or pressured to enroll in alternative programs[114]

- A requirement that a doctor verify every six weeks that the student can remain in school[115]

- Refusal to let a pregnant student register[116]

109. Michael L. Williams, *Federal Agency Fights Discrimination Against Pregnant Students,* YOUTH LAW NEWS, January–February 1992, at 10.

110. In author's files, OCR docket # 09-00-1323.

111. In author's files, OCR docket # 07-99-2138, 07-99-2113, 10-93-1119, and 06-99-2252.

112. In author's files, OCR docket # 06-99-2008.

113. In author's files, OCR docket # 04-99-2135.

114. In author's files, OCR docket # 06-98-5002.

115. In author's files, OCR docket # 06-98-5002.

116. In author's files, OCR docket # 02-97-2012.

- Failure to appoint a Title IX compliance officer or adopt and publicize a grievance policy[117]

- Counseling pregnant and parenting students to leave school and seek a GED[118]

- Refusal to accept pregnant students in an electronics training program[119]

- Dismissal from an apprenticeship program due to pregnancy[120]

- Barring female students with children from extracurricular activities[121]

- Refusal to treat medically necessary absences for pregnancy, childbirth and recovery as excused[122]

- Removing pregnant students from physical education classes until they present a doctor's certificate (when this was not the procedure for other students with temporary disability)[123]

- Rules that married students and unwed mothers may not hold offices, leadership positions, represent the school or take part in activities[124]

PREGNANT STUDENTS AS CHILDREN WITH SPECIAL NEEDS

In 1974 the North Carolina General Assembly recognized special educational needs, declaring it our state policy "to ensure every child a fair and full opportunity to reach his full potential and that no child as defined in this

117. In author's files, OCR docket # 06-97-2133.
118. In author's files, OCR docket # 06-97-1477.
119. In author's files, OCR docket # 05-96-2111.
120. In author's files, OCR docket # 04-96-2036.
121. In author's files, OCR docket # 04-93-1229.
122. In author's files, OCR docket # 15-92-4002.
123. In author's files, OCR Compliance Review # 05-92-5002.
124. In author's files, OCR Compliance Review # 01-91-5003.

act shall be excluded from service or education for any reason whatsoever."[125] Pregnant students were included from the beginning in the legislative definition of children who may have special needs,[126] and they are still included.[127] When the federal government enacted similar legislation the next year, however, it did not—and still does not—define them as children with disabilities.[128] As a result, North Carolina receives no federal funds to provide special education services to pregnant students.

Despite the General Assembly's action in 1974, the Department of Public Instruction's Division for Exceptional Children declined to treat students as having special educational needs because they were pregnant.[129] Although two attorney general's letters concluded that the state's responsibility for pregnant children is the same as for others covered by the statute,[130] DPI instructed school districts to treat only the exceptional pregnant student as a

125. 1973 N.C. Sess. Laws ch. 1293. The current formulation is that the state has a duty to provide all children with special needs a free appropriate public education. G.S. 115C-107.

126. 1973 N.C. Sess. Laws ch. 1293, Sec. 4.

127. "The term 'children with special needs' includes, without limitation, all children from age five through twenty who because of permanent or temporary mental, physical or emotional handicaps need special education, are unable to have all their needs met in a regular class without special education or related services, or are unable to be adequately educated in the public schools. It includes those who are . . . pregnant. . . ." G.S. 115C-109.

128. 20 U.S.C. § 1401(3).

129. Susan M. Presti and Blanche Glimps, *Pregnant Teenagers: Their Education is Suffering*, 4 N.C. INSIGHT, September 1981, 2–9, at 4–6. The authors quote the director of the Division for Exceptional Children: "A child must be handicapped as well as pregnant in order to qualify for special services"; and the Division's information specialist: "I don't have anything to do with pregnant girls. . . . [They] do not fall within the Division for Exceptional Children. They are not part of our jurisdiction. I don't understand the reasoning [for including them in the Creech Bill.]." (quotations at 5).

130. Letter to Ruby Milgrom, Chairman, Governor's Advocacy Council on Children and Youth, September 30, 1980; Letter to Theodore R. Drain, Director, Division for Exceptional Children, June 25, 1981.

child with special needs.[131] *Education Law in North Carolina* described DPI's position and the resulting situation in public schools:

> State law governing children with special needs specifically includes pregnant girls within the definition of children with special needs. Nevertheless, actual practice through the state, on the basis of advice given to local school systems by the Department of Public Instruction, is that only those pregnant students who request specialized instruction or are identified as having other special needs actually receive special services.[132]

The tension between state law and actual practice in the state still exists, presenting a problem for school administrators and attorneys. The statutory description of children with special needs fits many or, more likely, most pregnant students—"children . . . who because of . . . temporary physical or emotional handicaps need special education, are unable to have all their needs met in a regular class without special education or related services, or are unable to be adequately educated in the public schools."[133] The statutory list of specific conditions qualifying a child as one with special needs includes "pregnant."[134] Moreover, recent efforts to remove pregnant students from the special needs category failed,[135] although LEAs need not prepare an in-

---

131. *Questions and Answers about Exceptional Children: A Handbook for Educational Administrators*, Raleigh, N.C.: Division for Exceptional Children, N.C. Department of Public Instruction (Summer 1982), at 16.

132. NORMAN ACKER, *Health Law*, in EDUCATION LAW IN NORTH CAROLINA at 22-10 (Robert Phay ed., Chapel Hill, N.C., Institute of Government 1988). This chapter is not included in the current (2003) edition. It could be obtained by contacting Janine Murphy, Principals Executive Program, Chapel Hill, N.C. Murphy is the current editor of *Education Law in North Carolina*.

133. G.S. 115C-109.

134. *Id.*

135. Senate Bill 927, 2001–2002 Session, and House Bill 318, 2003–2004 Session.

dividualized educational program (IEP) for them.[136] In place of the IEP, a statute directs the State Board of Education to adopt rules on an "educational program for the pregnant children."[137] Another statute, about diagnosing and evaluating pregnant students, tells the State Board to "focus on the particular needs of the pregnant child."[138] A third provision states, "Each local educational agency shall prepare educational programs for the pregnant children. The State Board of Education shall promulgate rules . . . to address the preparation of these educational programs, which . . . include specific standards for ensuring that *the individual educational needs of each [pregnant] child* are addressed." (emphasis added)[139] In sum, North Carolina law requires that (1) LEAs must recognize that for most students pregnancy is likely to create educational needs; (2) LEAs may not ignore those needs; and (3) LEAs must assess and address those needs individually, case by case.

The position of the State Board/DPI[140] is different and so is practice in many LEAs. The Board has not adopted standards for meeting individual needs, as required by statute. Instead, the Board transferred its obligation to LEAs, telling them to "prepare and implement a written program to meet

---

136. G.S. 115C-113(f). The 1983 General Assembly removed the requirement of an IEP for pregnant and academically gifted students.

137. G.S. 115C-110(d)(2) instructs the State Board of Education to adopt rules covering "[m]inimum standards for the . . . educational program for the pregnant children, who receive special education and related services. . . ." Without the comma the provision would reinforce DPI's position by referring to only a subset of pregnant students as having special needs. With the comma, however, the provision refers to all pregnant students, describing them as eligible for special education and related services.

138. G.S. 115C-113(a).

139. G.S. 115C-113(h).

140. Sections .1501(A)(9), .1505(D)(7), and (E)(12), *Procedures Governing Programs and Services for Children with Disabilities* (revised August 3, 2000) (hereafter *Procedures*).

the special educational needs of pregnant students."[141] The ACLU-NC survey found that half of LEAs have no written policy or standards. Moreover, DPI no longer requires LEAs to include pregnant students in the annual count of students with special needs.[142]

At this time, the only significant benefit a pregnant student receives under state exceptional children law is the right to instruction at home if she is medically unable to attend school. Such a student fits the State Board/DPI definition of pregnant students with special needs.[143] North Carolina statute promises a child with special needs "a free appropriate public education." DPI expresses the entitlement more specifically, as "specially designed instruction, at no cost to the parent, to meet the unique needs of the child with a disability, including . . . home instruction."[144] DPI also advises LEAs, "In providing services to a child with special educational needs, the first factor should be the degree to which the child will benefit from such an arrangement rather than administrative considerations."[145] As a result, there seems to be general agreement that the State Board mandate that an "LEA shall prepare and implement a written program to meet the special needs of pregnant students"[146] must include providing home instruction in such cases.

Because the legal obligation to treat pregnant students as children with special needs does not exist at the federal level, and is not well-defined or enforced at the state level, local school administrators may hesitate to adopt

141. 16 NCAC 6H.0107(6) and Policy ID Number HSP-D-005, "Special Education Assessment and Placement Procedures, *North Carolina State Board of Education Policy Manual*, August 3, 2000.

142. Telephone conversation with representative of DPI Division of Exceptional Children, September 12, 2002.

143. Pregnant students with special needs are those who, because of their pregnancy, require special education and/or related services other than those which can be provided through regular education services." Section .1501, "Definitions," (A)(9), *Procedures*, at 3.

144. Section .1501 "Definitions," N, *Procedures*, at 15.

145. Section .1510 "Continuum of Programs and Services—Least Restrictive Environment," C, *Procedures*, 52.

146. 16 NCAC 6H.0107(d)(6).

policy in this area. Another possibility, however, is to take the initiative. Good practice might be, on learning that a girl is pregnant, to meet with her (and her parents if she is under eighteen and unmarried) to offer assistance with planning how she can continue her education through and after her pregnancy. This could be an opportunity to anticipate and avoid excessive absences and to discuss (being careful not to discriminate on the basis of pregnancy) all the educational options available should the girl elect them. To the extent that a plan is developed the school will have provided the student with individual consideration of her educational needs in a nondiscriminatory fashion.

ENROLLMENT

The Right to Enroll

State law provides that anyone in North Carolina under age twenty-one who has not been removed from school for cause and who does not have a high school diploma is entitled to attend public school.[147] Also, the federal law known as Title IX (described above) ensures that pregnant students, assuming they are otherwise eligible, can enroll. Moreover, on constitutional principles, a school almost certainly could not refuse to enroll all students who are married or are parents.

Where Pregnant and Parenting Minors May Enroll

Some pregnant or parenting students present unusual enrollment issues. A few are told to leave home, or choose to, without their parents making a suitable arrangement for them with family friends, relatives, in a maternity home, or elsewhere.[148] Such a minor may become homeless, either living in

147. G.S. 115C-366(a).

148. Inquiry from R.N./Maternity Care Coordinator, Guilford County Health Department, July 28, 2000; interview with Ann Arant and Jenette Hodge, Johnston County Department of Social Services, Smithfield, N.C., October 17, 2000. *See also* Anne Dellinger, "Social Services for Pregnant and Parenting Adolescents," *NCMB Forum*, No. 3 (2002), 14–15.

a shelter[149] or on her own.[150] (See following section.) Or, even when parents place a child in a new district, the school may not consider her eligible to be enrolled there because her parents live elsewhere.

State statute makes local boards responsible for enrolling students.[151] The general rule is that students have a right to enroll where they are domiciled,[152] and a minor's domicile is that of the person legally responsible for him or her—generally, the minor's parents. Several North Carolina decisions on school enrollment make it clear that unemancipated minors, wherever they may be living, keep the domicile of their parents,[153] and there is a state statute

149. Shelter staff in North Carolina report seeing very few pregnant or parenting teens although they are overrepresented among homeless youth (see paper cited in next note). A shelter director observes, though, that staff might easily miss pregnancy in dealing with other problems. Telephone conversation with Michael Rieder, Exec. Director, Haven House, Raleigh, N.C., March 5, 2001.

150. Approximately half of homeless youth are girls. Some of these leave home due to pregnancy, and others become pregnant—and often parents—as a result of sexual assault or prostitution following homelessness. *Homeless and Runaway Youth Health and Health Needs: A Position Paper of the Society for Adolescent Medicine*, 31 J. OF ADOL. H. 717–726 (1992).

151. G.S. 115C-366, "Assignment of student to a particular school," is the primary statute.

152. G.S. 115C-366(a). Domicile is a person's permanent, established home, as opposed to a temporary place of residence. Hall v. Board of Elections, 280 N.C. 600, 605, 187 S.E.2d 52, 55 (1972). To establish domicile, a person must be physically present in a place and intend to make a permanent home there (but not necessarily at the same time). Once domicile is established, one may reside elsewhere for extended periods without losing it. Legal writers describe domicile as a matter of fact and intent, Horne v. Horne, 31 N.C. (9 Ired.) 99 (1848), which can be indicated by various direct and circumstantial evidence—paying taxes, for example; voting; declaring one's intent to be a domiciliary; taking part in community affairs.

153. Graham v. Mock, 143 N.C. App. 315, 545 S.E.2d 263 (2001), *appeal dismissed, review denied*, 353 N.C. 726, 550 S.E.2d 776 (2001). The fourteen-year-old plaintiff was threatened with sexual assault in her Chicago neighborhood. Her mother sent her for safety to an uncle in Davidson County who tried to enroll her. *See also* Craven County Bd. of Educ. v. Willoughby, 121 N.C. App. 495, 466 S.E.2d 334 (1996); Chapel Hill–Carrboro City Schools System v. Chavioux, 116 N.C. App. 131, 446 S.E.2d 612 (1994).

to the same effect.[154] Students aged eighteen to twenty-one and the few minors who are emancipated may establish their own domicile.

There are exceptions. Certain minors can attend school, without paying tuition, in the district they live in, although their parents live elsewhere. The following groups, among others,[155] are eligible:

- Those living in child care institutions, such as foster homes, group homes, or maternity homes[156]

- Those who are homeless or whose parents are homeless[157]

- Those living with an adult domiciliary because of (1) a parent or legal guardian's death, serious illness, or incarceration; (2) a parent or legal guardian's abuse, neglect, or abandonment of the student;[158] (3) a parent or guardian having a physical or mental condition resulting in inability to care for or supervise the student adequately; or (4) the student's home being lost or rendered uninhabitable by natural disaster[159]

- Those who are children with special needs,[160] a category that includes many pregnant students

154. G.S. 115C-366.2.

155. G.S. 115C-366(c); G.S. 115C-366.2.

156. G.S. 115C-366(a1); G.S. 155C-111; Craven County Bd. of Educ. v. Willoughby, 121 N.C. App. 495, 466 S.E.2d 334 (1996).

157. G.S. 115C-366(a2) defines "homeless" as lacking "a fixed, regular, and adequate nighttime residence," living in a shelter, or using a sleeping accommodation not ordinarily used by humans.

158. Abandonment means relinquishing "complete control of the student as evidenced by the failure to provide substantial support and parental guidance." There must have been an adjudication of abuse or neglect and, if the State Board of Education has adopted definitions, those must be satisfied as well. G.S. 115C-366(a3).

159. The person with whom the child resides and, in most cases, his parent or guardian must submit affidavits to the school board about the child's eligibility. G.S. 115C-366(a3).

160. G.S. 115C-111; see also Craven County Bd. of Educ. v. Willoughby, 121 N.C. App. 495, 466 S.E.2d 334 (1996).

Enrolling Homeless Minors

Homeless children and youth—especially those who are pregnant or parenting —badly need schools' help. Transportation to and from school is a major problem for them, as is some LEAs' mistaken insistence that parents must reside in the district and students must have documentation of various kinds in order to enroll. Homeless youth are hard to help, however, because, by definition, they are hard to find[161] and track.[162] Even their total numbers are unknown. Estimates for the United States vary from 500,000[163] to 930,000.[164] North Carolina's data too are imprecise. North Carolina is one of six states that did not provide, for inclusion in the U.S. Department of Education (DOE) 2000 report to Congress, the number of homeless students enrolled nor the number attending school regularly.[165] (However, DOE acknowledged that most of the other states' numbers were likely mere estimates.) Instead, North Carolina submitted estimates for students by age groupings and a total estimate of 6,787 homeless students in the state.[166] According to DPI, better

161. The U.S. Department of Education urges school liaisons to identify homeless children and youth both in and out of school by communicating with shelters, soup kitchens, food banks, transitional living programs, street outreach teams, drop-in centers, local departments of social services, housing agencies, health departments, and faith-based institutions. *Education for Homeless Children and Youth Program: Non-regulatory Guidance,* Washington, D.C.: U.S. Department of Education (March 2003), at 8. Available at http://www.ed.gov/programs/homeless/ guidance.doc.

162. *School Can Help Anchor a Life That's In Flux: Q & A with Ann Fisher, Durham schools' liaison for homeless students,* THE NEWS & OBSERVER (Raleigh, N.C.) August 27, 2003, 7B, Cols. 2–4. Fisher sees ". . . children who aren't of legal age but who aren't staying with a legal guardian. They could be couch surfing, camping out or sleeping in cars."

163. The total number the states reported for 2000 to the federal education agency. U.S. Department of Education, *2000 Report to Congress on Homeless Education,* at 14. Report available at http://www.ed.gov/programs/homeless/ rpt2000.doc.

164. The estimate of the U.S. Department of Education, *id.* at 9.

165. *Id.* at 4–5.

166. *Id.* at 14. The figure seems low for the 11th most populous state, which has a significant number of migrant farm workers and now the fastest-growing Latino population in the United States, some of whom are minors immigrating without their parents. (See definition of *unaccompanied youth,* note 171, below).

numbers should be forthcoming now that federal law (described below) requires each LEA to appoint a liaison for homeless students.[167]

In addition to the state law described above and the state plan for educating homeless children and youth,[168] there is extensive federal legal protection for them.[169] In 2002 Congress reauthorized legislation on the rights of homeless students (the McKinney-Vento Homeless Assistance Act), adding important requirements and emphasizing the needs of homeless unaccompanied youth.[170] As a federal law McKinney-Vento controls contrary state and local law, policy, and practice.

The act defines *homeless, enroll, enrollment*, and *unaccompanied youth*[171] (a category that includes some pregnant and parenting minors), and requires the following:

- States must provide homeless youth the same free public education offered to others. This means comparable access, in addition to the regular program, to transportation; services for disadvantaged students, children with special needs, and students with limited English proficiency; vocational education; programs for gifted and talented students; and school meal programs.

- States must review and begin to alter law, regulation, practice, or policy that may hamper homeless youth's enrollment, attendance, or success in school.

167. Telephone conversation with Cynthia Floyd, Interim Liaison for Homeless Education, N.C. Department of Public Instruction, December 16, 2002.

168. Policy ID Number EEO-I-000, *North Carolina State Board of Education Policy Manual*, adopted November 5, 1998. The manual is available at http://www.ncpublicschools.org.

169. Subtitle B, Education for Homeless Children and Youth, Sections 721–726 of the McKinney-Vento Homeless Assistance Act, as reauthorized Jan 2002, codified at 42 U.S.C. § 11431-11435. Regulations are at 67 F.R. 10,697 (March 8, 2002).

170. *Education for Homeless Children and Youth Program: Non-regulatory Guidance*, Washington, D.C.: U.S. Department of Education, (March 2003). Available at http://www.ed.gov/programs/homeless/guidance.doc.

171. "The term *unaccompanied youth* includes a youth not in the physical custody of a parent or guardian." 42 U.S.C. § 11434a.

- Schools and school districts must not segregate students from the mainstream or stigmatize them because they are homeless. Districts and schools must allow them access to education and other services needed for academic success.[172]

- Schools must immediately enroll homeless youth even if they are unaccompanied and do not have the records normally required (proof of residency, birth or guardianship certificates, academic records, and immunization records among others).[173]

- Every school district must name as liaison for homeless students a staff person who is to be responsible for helping them enroll and succeed.[174] For example, the liaison must inform homeless youth of their rights to transportation (including to their school of origin) and rights to appeal decisions on school assignment and have the matter promptly resolved. The liaison is also to assist students in pursuing their rights.

- At the request of a parent or the liaison, states must ensure that, when feasible and in the youth's best interest, LEAs transport a homeless youth to and from the school he or she attended when not homeless or in which he or she last enrolled.[175]

- Each state must submit a plan describing its efforts to DOE.[176]

ASSIGNMENT

What school a student attends and how she is placed in a program or grade are largely governed by state statute. The local board of education assigns children to a school.[177] While assignment is usually based on residence, it

172. 42 U.S.C. § 11431 and 11432(e)(3).
173. 42 U.S.C. § 11432(g)(3)(C).
174. 42 U.S.C. § 11432(g)(6).
175. 42 U.S.C. § 11431(g)(3).
176. 42 U.S.C. § 11432(g).
177. G.S. 115C-366(b).

can be made "for any other reason which the board of education in its sole discretion deems sufficient," except exclusion because of race, creed, color, or national origin.[178] A parent, guardian, or person standing in loco parentis may appeal the assignment, first to the board[179] and then to superior court.[180] Within a school the principal has "authority to grade and classify pupils," based on academic criteria and the student's "best educational interests."[181]

For pregnant and parenting students, Title IX and federal constitutional law also play roles. As noted earlier, Title IX regulations forbid schools to exclude pregnant students from any class, program, or activity unless the student voluntarily asks for a different placement.[182] In that case the school must ensure that the new placement "is comparable to that offered to non-pregnant students."[183] As for young parents, a school cannot, on the basis of sex, "[s]ubject any person to separate or different rules of behavior, sanctions, or other treatment"[184]—a provision that protects young mothers from worse treatment than fathers. Finally, constitutional principles of due process and equal protection would prevent a principal from, for example, making all parenting students drop college preparatory courses and extracurricular activities and enroll in vocational training.

ATTENDANCE

Many pregnant—and even more parenting—students struggle to attend classes and do homework in order to earn academic credit. Indeed, professionals who work with them often identify maintaining school work as the

178. G.S. 115C-367.
179. G.S. 115C-369.
180. G.S. 115C-370.
181. G.S. 115C-288(a).
182. 34 C.F.R. § 106.40(b)(1).
183. 34 C.F.R. § 106.40(b)(3).
184. 34 C.F.R. § 106.31(b)(4).

most pressing problem.[185] The State Board of Education recognizes the high risk that these students will fail and urges schools to offer them dropout prevention services.[186]

Legal aspects of attendance include these issues:

- Whether married students must attend school
- Title IX's requirement that certain absences be excused for pregnant students
- How to appeal to reclassify unexcused absences as excused
- Entitlement to homebound instruction
- How a school should handle a student's absence to go to court seeking a waiver of parental consent to abortion

Compulsory Attendance

Unmarried students must remain in school until age sixteen,[187] but North Carolina schools are treating married students differently. Attorney general's opinions state[188]—and many North Carolina attorneys assume—that married students under sixteen are free to leave school because no one has authority to stop them. This legal conclusion is based on the facts that our

185. Interview with Gloria Rentrope, UNC Hospitals social worker, Chapel Hill, N.C., June 6, 1996; interview with Ann Arant and Jenette Hodge, codirectors, Adolescent Parenting Program, Johnston County, Smithfield, N.C., October 17, 2000.

186. Policy ID Number HSP-Q-001, "Policy regarding guidelines and definitions of a student at risk, alternative programs, and alternative school," *North Carolina State Board of Education Policy Manual.* Available at http://sbepolicy. dpi.state.nc.us.

187. "Every parent, guardian or other person in this State having charge or control of a child between the ages of seven and sixteen years shall cause such child to attend school. . . ." G.S. 115C-378.

188. Opinion Letters from Andrew A. Vanore Jr. to E.M. White, Superintendent, Caldwell County Schools (April 21, 1969) and to Wayne Collier, Assistant Superintendent, Cumberland County Schools (December 16, 1969).

compulsory attendance statute is addressed to parents; married minors are deemed emancipated;[189] and parents do not control emancipated children.

No court has ruled on the matter, however, and in the author's opinion at least two other views of the law are possible. First, to be emancipated is to assume the duties of an adult. Because the public policy favoring compulsory attendance is so strong, those who enforce it might assume that emancipation transfers the duty to educate a child from parent to child, so that an emancipated minor himself or herself has a legal duty to stay in school until age sixteen. A second possibility is that emancipation does not include exemption from compulsory attendance. For example, the state and federal restrictions on youth employment, enforced by the U.S. and North Carolina Departments of Labor, apply to *all* minors including emancipated minors.

Perhaps the best argument for the current interpretation of compulsory attendance—that married fourteen- and fifteen-year-olds may quit school—lies in the fact that the compulsory attendance statute has criminal penalties. It is generally agreed that criminal laws should be interpreted narrowly, so that people do not break the law unknowingly, and the narrowest interpretation is that the law applies only to parents of students. Given these strong, competing considerations it would be useful to have the law clarified through amendment or judicial interpretation.

Excused and Unexcused Absences

Title IX regulations require schools to excuse absences caused by certain conditions for "so long a period of time as is deemed medically necessary by the student's physician, at the conclusion of which the student shall be reinstated to the status which she held when the leave began."[190] The conditions are pregnancy, childbirth, false pregnancy, termination of pregnancy, or recovery from any of these. Title IX says nothing about absences due to

---

189. Marriage emancipates a minor, and fourteen- and fifteen-year-olds who are pregnant, are expecting a child, or are parents may marry with judicial permission. G.S. 51-2.1(a).

190. 34 C.F.R. § 106.40(b)(5).

parenting. If Title IX and North Carolina law conflict, Title IX controls because it is federal law. Therefore, school administrators violate Title IX if they refuse to grant excused absences for the conditions named above.

There is a serious problem in the state process for determining which absences are excused (for any student, not only pregnant or parenting students). The problem is that the State Board's regulations on excused absences[191] are not consistent with the state statute that authorizes principals or superintendents to excuse temporary absences for "sickness or other unavoidable cause."[192] The statute says school administrators may excuse any absence unless the State Board has said it is an "unlawful" absence. The State Board, however, defines as unlawful any absence of more than half a school day that the State Board does not identify as an absence that must be excused.[193] In short, the State Board purports to largely deprive school officials of the discretion granted by statute. In addition, the State Board's list of lawful absences[194] is so restrictive that principals and superintendents cannot excuse absences that most reasonable people would agree are justified.[195] This places local officials in a dilemma and doubtless results in some students accumulating unexcused absences they can ill afford.

191. 16 NCAC 6E.0102.

192. G.S. 115C-378.

193. Division of School Business, N.C. Department of Public Instruction, *School Attendance and Student Accounting Manual,* Chapter 2, Section IV, "Attendance," Subsections D (Lawful Absences) and H (Unlawful Absences), October 2003 (hereafter *School Attendance and Student Accounting*). Available at http://www.ncpublicschools.org/fbs/sasa/ch2.htm.

194. The list is as follows: illness or injury rendering the student physically unable to attend school; quarantine or isolation; death in the immediate family; medical or dental appointments; court or administrative proceedings; religious observance; and educational opportunity for which prior approval was obtained. *School Attendance and Student Accounting,* Ch. 2, IV, D.

195. Under the State Board regulation, for example, officials could not excuse the following absences if a student were out more than half a school day: being at the bedside of a dying parent or, particularly relevant to parenting students, tending to a sick child; being under suicide watch at home; attending an immediate family member's wedding; or traveling with parents taking a sibling for major surgery.

As for pregnant and parenting students, at least the State Board classifies them as "at risk,"[196] and schools may allow at-risk students to make up absences during non-school hours. This may benefit the student and also allows the LEA to count the student as in attendance for purposes of the district's state funding (Average Daily Membership).

Homebound Instruction and Absence to Seek a Waiver of Parental Consent to Abortion

Homebound Instruction

Many pregnant students receive instruction at home before and after childbirth. A few experience complications that make such instruction medically necessary for a prolonged period. Once a student has met in person with school personnel to arrange for homebound instruction, she is counted present throughout the period during which services are delivered.[197]

Absence to Seek a Waiver of Parental Consent to Abortion

North Carolina law requires that before a minor has an abortion, the physician must have consent from the minor and a parent (or parent figure).[198] As an alternative, a minor may secure permission from a judge to make her own decision about abortion. This process is called petitioning for waiver of parental consent to abortion, and in most judicial districts it requires the minor to visit the courthouse more than once and perhaps keep other appointments. For example, before her hearing before the judge, she may need to meet with an attorney or guardian ad litem appointed to advise her. All absences for these purposes are excused, because LEAs must excuse absences caused by a student's being a party to a court procedure.[199]

Confidentiality is very important for absences associated with a judicial waiver. The U.S. Supreme Court has held that states that limit minors' rights

196. Policy ID Number HSP-Q-001, "Policy regarding guidelines and definitions of a student at risk, alternative programs, and alternative school," *North Carolina State Board of Education Policy Manual,* IV, F (January 13, 2000).

197. *School Attendance and Student Accounting,* Ch. 2, IV, C.

198. G.S. 90-21.7.

199. 16 NCAC 06E.0102(a)(5).

with respect to abortion by requiring notice to or consent from parents must establish a confidential procedure through which a minor can seek a waiver of the parental involvement requirement.[200] By confidential, the Court means that the procedure may not identify the minor, which includes not telling her parents that she has petitioned. To comply with the U.S. Supreme Court ruling, North Carolina law requires court personnel to protect the identity of any minor seeking a waiver.[201] Although no law on abortion— federal or state—mentions schools, for public schools to reveal to parents that their daughter has petitioned a court would seem to violate the intent of the Supreme Court requirement that states establish a confidential waiver procedure. Breaching the student's confidence might also violate Title IX's prohibition against pregnancy discrimination.

In at least one North Carolina county, after a hearing on a judicial waiver the clerk of court gives the minor a letter telling school officials not to ask why she was absent and not to reveal her absence to parents or others.[202] There is no legal requirement that an LEA notify a parent of such an absence or include in a student's file the reason for it. Noting only that an excused absence occurred might prevent parents learning from the file that their daughter had asked for a waiver.

Appeals to Reclassify Absences As Excused

While LEAs have various policies on excusing absences and granting credit, the thrust of the state ABCs program[203] and the federal No Child Left Behind legislation[204] is to keep students in school, help them succeed, and graduate them

200. Bellotti v. Baird, 443 U.S. 622 (1979).

201. G.S. 90-21.8.

202. American Civil Liberties Union training manual, in author's files.

203. School-Based Management and Acccountability Program, 1996 N.C. Sess. Laws ch. 716, 1995-3 (codified as amended at G.S. 115C-105.20 through 115C-105.41, 2003). The program seeks to improve student performance, make schools safer, and keep parents informed.

204. Pub. L. No. 107-110, 115 Stat. 1425 (2002) (codified primarily at 20 U.S.C. § 6301-6578). This legislation, which is similar in purpose to the ABCs program, penalizes schools whose students do not show measurable progress, requires certain teacher qualifications, and emphasizes school safety and informing parents.

as productive members of the community. Pregnant students may need assistance to meet these goals. Often they accumulate absences early in the pregnancy; for example, before it is known or acknowledged, while decisions are made about whether to continue it, and while health care is sought.[205] By the time these matters are settled, the student may find she has exceeded the allowable number of absences.

At that point it may be appropriate for a student to ask to make up the work missed and ask that the absences be reclassified as excused. If school officials deny the request, she can appeal to the school board. A student may appeal a school's final administrative decision[206] to the board when the decision is an "alleged violation of a specified federal law" and, if the appeal to the board is unsuccessful, may appeal to superior court.[207] In this case, the statute would be Title IX, which forbids discrimination on the basis of pregnancy and treats pregnancy like other temporary disabilities. In addition to the statutory right, most LEAs have a policy on absences and grading, which usually contains an appeals process. Many such policies allow students whose absences are excused to make up work for grading purposes.

THE HEALTH CURRICULUM

At least 80 percent of minors' pregnancies are unintended.[208] To prevent unintended pregnancy and adverse health effects, health and education experts report that students, including those already pregnant or parenting, need accurate

205. Interview with Gloria Rentrope, note 185.

206. Defined as "a decision of a school employee from which no further appeal to a school administrator is available." G.S. 115C-45(c).

207. G.S. 115C-45(c).

208. The rate is 81.7 percent in girls under fifteen; 82.7 percent in young women fifteen to seventeen. Stanley K. Henshaw, *Unintended Pregnancy in the United States*, 30 FAMILY PLANNING PERSPECTIVES (January/February 1998). North Carolina's percentage may be higher; 76.6 percent of new mothers under twenty said their pregnancy was unintended. Kevin H. Gross, *Unintended Pregnancies in North Carolina: Results from the North Carolina PRAMS Survey*, SCHS STUDIES, No. 136 (Raleigh, N.C.), Nov. 2002.

information on these subjects: contraception, options after a pregnancy diagnosis, parenting, adoption, and related issues.[209] Many U.S. schools no longer offer the information. One reason is that the federal government offers states more than $100 million annually for teaching abstinence.[210] Other federal education funds can be used for sex education so long as it includes abstinence and excludes distribution of contraceptives.[211] School districts in the South are considerably more likely to teach only abstinence than LEAs elsewhere.[212]

Since 1995 few North Carolina adolescents have heard complete information about reproductive health at school. The School Health Education Act[213] adopted that year

209. David Satcher, *The Surgeon General's Call to Action to Promote Sexual Health and Responsible Sexual Behavior,* Washington, D.C.: U.S. Department of Health and Human Services (June 2001), at 11–13; *Comprehensive Child Health Plan: 2000–2005; Report to the North Carolina Department of Health and Human Services,* Chapel Hill, N.C.: North Carolina Institute of Medicine (May 23, 2000), at 25 (hereafter *NCIOM Report*); Susan Black, *Facts of Life,* THE AMERICAN SCHOOL BOARD JOURNAL 33–36 (August 1998); Catherine Gewertz, *Clear, Consistent Messages Help Deter Teen Pregnancy, Study Finds,* EDUCATION WEEK (June 6, 2001); National Association of School Nurses, *Position Statement: Adolescent Parents* (Revised 1997), available at http://www.nasn.org/positions/positions.htm.

210. $50 million through welfare legislation; $12 million through the Adolescent Family Life program; and $40 million through the Maternal and Child Health Block grant. *Abstinence Education Programs,* 7 WELFARE INFORMATION NETWORK (January 2003). Available at http://www.financeprojectinfo.org/publications/abstinenceeducation.htm.

211. 20 U.S.C. § 7906.

212. *Fact Sheet: Sexuality and Abstinence Education Policies in U.S. Public School Districts,* The Alan Guttmacher Institute (1999). Available at http://www.agi-usa.org/pubs/factsheet_121399.html.

213. G.S. 115C-81(e1). For analyses of the legislation, see Anne Dellinger, *Parental Rights and School Health: North Carolina's Legislation,* 28 SCHOOL LAW BULLETIN 1–9 (Chapel Hill, N.C., Institute of Government, Winter 1997), and *NC's Abstinence Curriculum: Some Answers,* available at http://www.ncpublic schools.org/curriculum/health/abstinenceqa.html.

- requires abstinence-until-marriage education;[214]

- instructs the State Board of Education to develop teaching objectives for sexually transmitted disease prevention that emphasize abstinence, monogamy, and the legal status of homosexual acts;[215] and

- lets parents and the public review materials and comment before school districts may offer broader instruction.[216]

About a dozen of the 117 districts supplement the state curriculum.[217]

As an alternative to classroom instruction, a growing number of adolescents use the Internet for reproductive health information,[218] but Internet access is linked to race and income. In one survey, 80 percent of non-Hispanic whites, 66 percent of African-Americans, and 55 percent of Hispanics had Internet access at home.[219] Some students without Internet access at home gain access through public libraries,[220] but Congress may have inadvertently limited that possibility when it conditioned libraries' Internet funds on their preventing children's access to pornography and similar material.[221] Software intended to block pornography can substantially

214. G.S. 115C-81(e1)(1)l.

215. G.S. 115C-81(e1)(3). Following a U.S. Supreme Court decision [Lawrence v. Texas, _ U.S. _, 123 S. Ct. 2472, 156 L. Ed. 2d 508 (2003)] homosexual acts in private between consenting adults are legal.

216. G.S. 115C-81(e1)(6) and (7).

217. Artie Kamiya, former chief, DPI Healthful Living Section, cited in T. Keung Hui, *Wake may expand discussion topics in sex ed classes*, NEWS &OBSERVER (Raleigh, N.C.), March 22, 2002.

218. Kaiser Family Foundation, *Generation Rx.com: How Young People Use the Internet for Health Information*, Pub. #3202 (December 2001). Available at http://www.kff.org.

219. *Id.* at 19, Chart No. 18.

220. Ninety-five percent of U.S. libraries offer a connection and 10 percent of Internet users gain access by this means. Charles Lane, *Ruling Backs Porn Filters in Libraries*, WASHINGTON POST, June 23, 2003, p.A1.

221. Children's Internet Protection Act, 20 U.S.C.§ 9134, upheld in United States v. American Library Association, 539 U.S. 194 (2003).

interfere with access to reputable health Web sites.[222] Access is not the only problem with the Internet as a health resource. The accuracy, specificity, and relevance of information vary from one Web site to another. The incomplete health curriculum offered in nearly all North Carolina public schools and the lack of a consistent alternative for many students no doubt increase their desire for confidential communications with counselors, teachers, nurses, and other school staff. The legal status of these communications is discussed in the next two sections.

HEALTH CARE PROVIDED IN SCHOOLS

State law contains numerous references to student health. These are the provisions most relevant to pregnancy and parenting:

- The Basic Education program requires schools to instruct students in health[223] and to offer health services.[224]

- The curriculum must include information on specified health topics between kindergarten and ninth grade including family living, abstinence until marriage, preventing sexually transmitted disease and disease control.[225]

- Contraceptives may not be made available on school property.[226]

222. Caroline R. Richardson et al., *Does Pornography-Blocking Software Block Access to Health Information on the Internet?* 288 JAMA 2887–2894 (December 11, 2002).
223. G.S. 115C-81(a1).
224. G.S. 115C-81(b) says schools must offer "required support programs." The state administrative code (16 NCAC 6D.0401 and .0402) and State Board of Education Policy ID Number HSP-G-006 require school health services.
225. G.S. 115C-81(e1)(1).
226. G.S. 115C-81(e1)(9).

- The State Board of Education must see that LEAs provide services to children with special needs, including health services, that will allow them to stay in school.[227]

Federal and state disability law require schools to undertake other health efforts for some students. A state statute mentions administering drugs and medication, first aid, emergency care, or life-saving techniques,[228] but those are not the only services that may be offered. North Carolina has forty-five school-based or school-linked health centers in twenty-six counties,[229] and averages[230] one nurse for every 2,047 students.[231] Although a state task force recommended one per 750 children, the present number improves on the 1/3000 ratio set by the Basic Education Plan and is a significant improvement since 1991 when North Carolina had one school nurse per 6,000 to 8,000 students.[232]

For more than a century it was recognized that many students lacked adequate health care but U.S. schools still limited the treatment they provided.[233] Modern physicians too sometimes oppose school health care for

227. G.S. 115C-110(a), conforming state law to the Individuals with Disabilities Education Act (originally, Education for All Handicapped Children Act), 20 U.S.C. § 1400 to 1420.

228. G.S. 115C-307(c).

229. Information from Marilyn Asay, School Nurse Consultant, Division of Public Health, N.C. Department of Health and Human Services, April 1, 2003. There are fewer clinics than three years ago. Bruce Buchanan, *School health clinics hard to find*, GREENSBORO NEWS & RECORD, October 10, 2000.

230. School systems vary widely on this point. Seven LEAs meet or better the 1 to 750 recommended ratio, but another has one nurse for 7,800 students and five LEAs have no school nurse. Information from Marilyn Asay, above.

231. *Id.*

232. John J. Schlitt, *Bringing Health to Schools: Policy Implications for Southern States,* Southern Governors' Association (1991), at 3 (hereafter Schlitt.).

233. According to an historian of American medicine,

[H]ealth services for school children shifted from environmental to individual concerns in the late nineteenth century and then ran into barriers imposed by private practitioners. In the mid-1800s the first

fear of competition. The *Greensboro News and Record* wrote in 2000, "Political pressure from physicians may be partially to blame for the scarcity of school clinic funding, even though the [North Carolina] Institute of Medicine advocates increased spending. Allen, a Guilford County school board member, said some doctors see the clinics as competition for paying customers."[234] There are other problems as well. A Southern Governors' Association task force on school health reported, "The status of school health programs around the South seems as fragile as the health of those they are designed to serve."[235] The task force pointed to inadequate funding, vocal opposition from a minority of the public, and the autonomy of local school districts.[236] The North Carolina Institute of Medicine agrees that "programs affecting the reproductive health of minors have been mired in controversy for years."[237]

Reproductive health, especially that of girls, continues to raise legal concerns for schools.[238] One question, asked soon after North Carolina's School Health Education Act became effective in 1995, was whether the act covered

---

efforts in schools sought to improve ventilation and heating and to eliminate overcrowding. The one medical service occasionally provided was smallpox vaccination. In the 1890s . . . school health programs became increasingly medical in their approach. . . . [T]he chief objective was to control communicable disease. . . . "Acutely conscious of the delicate sensibilities of the medical profession . . . the Health Department stressed that the school inspectors were to give no professional treatment." (citation omitted)

PAUL STARR, THE SOCIAL TRANSFORMATION OF AMERICAN MEDICINE at 187–188 (New York, Basic Books 1984).

234. Buchanan, note 229 above.

235. Schlitt at 2.

236. *Id.* at 4.

237. *NCIOM Report*, note 209 above, at 39.

238. In one incident, for example, a principal allegedly barred girls from school until they produced test results for pregnancy and sexually transmitted disease. Susan Saulby with Abby Goodnough, *Suit Says School Ordered Girls Tested for Diseases After Party*, NEW YORK TIMES, July 9, 2003. The New York Civil Liberties Union is representing the girls in a suit filed July 8, 2003, in U.S. District Court for the Southern District of New York.

(that is, restricted) nurses working in school-based health clinics. The attorney general's office issued an opinion saying no: "The statute does not regulate the matters which a school nurse may discuss with a student in the context of providing medical assistance to a student or the materials to which she may refer in that context."[239] The opinion also says that the "statute pertains to the content of the comprehensive school health education program," not to instruction outside it.

A more recent opinion discusses school board authority in the area of reproductive health and possible consequences of the decisions a board might make in the area. A school attorney asked the attorney general whether the board could forbid school nurses[240] from referring students to the health department without parental consent. The attorney general replied that a school board "has the authority to define and limit the scope of clinical services provided at the school."[241] However, the opinion urged the board to consider its own and the LEA's possible tort liability for failing to refer and the liability problem such a position might pose for a health department and its employees. Any or all of these parties could be liable if the school board required nurses to "provide students with incomplete information about the student's health options, particularly in the absence of exceptions for emergencies and for situations where the information is otherwise medically indicated."[242]

The opinion does not offer examples, but a health provider would likely be negligent if she failed to discuss contraception, including emergency contraception, with a student she knew to be sexually active. Similarly, a school

---

239. Edwin M. Speas Jr., Senior Deputy Attorney General, Thomas J. Ziko, Special Deputy Attorney General, and Laura C. Crumpler, Assistant Attorney General, to Richard L. Thompson, Deputy State Superintendent, Department of Public Instruction, November 3, 1997, quotations at 4.

240. The nurses were health department employees working in the schools under a contract between the LEA and the local health department.

241. Ann Reed, Senior Deputy Attorney General, and Gayl M. Manthei, Special Deputy Attorney General, to Koy E. Dawkins, Union County School Attorney, May 9, 2001, quotation at 1.

242. *Id.* at 2.

nurse's discussing childbirth, but not pregnancy termination could cause serious harm to a pregnant student who does not want to bear a child or for whom pregnancy presents serious health risks. The opinion stated that a health department supplying nurses to work in the school system might prefer to terminate its contract rather than risk liability for malpractice. It also repeated the earlier opinion's statement that the School Health Education Act does not apply to school nursing. Therefore, no law restricts what a nurse may say to a student whom she is diagnosing, treating, or counseling.

Minors can consent to prevention, diagnosis, and treatment of pregnancy, communicable disease, emotional disturbance, and substance abuse and can consent to abortion if a judge waives the parental consent requirement. For a fuller description of the law on reproductive health care for minors, see Anne Dellinger and Arlene Davis, *Health Care for Pregnant Adolescents: A Legal Guide* (Chapel Hill, N.C.: Institute of Government, 2001). Available at http://www.adolescentpregnancy.unc.edu. The book can be read and printed without charge from the Web site.

COUNSELING

North Carolina schools must offer counseling,[243] a service that is often crucial for pregnant and parenting students. "Counseling" here refers to the work of guidance counselors, social workers, and psychologists employed by the LEA or working under a contract.

Two legal issues that are particularly relevant to the valuable work counselors do with pregnant and parenting students are discussed in this section:

1. Does the School Health Education Act apply to and limit counselors?

2. To what extent is counseling confidential?

Neither question has an obvious answer.

243. 16 NCAC 6D. 0401 and State Board of Education Policy ID Number HSP-G-006.

An attorney general opinion (see the preceding section) states that the School Health Education Act does not cover school nurses when they confer with students as patients. The Act applies only when a nurse instructs students as part of the health curriculum.[244] Although the opinion mentions only nurses, its reasoning seems equally well fitted to guidance counselors, psychologists, social workers, or any other school staff member who advises individual students (as opposed to teaching students). In the author's opinion, school personnel are probably covered by the act only when teaching the health curriculum.[245]

The second question—how confidential is counseling—needs a longer discussion. Students seeking counseling about reproductive health are likely to care greatly about confidentiality and counselors would like to reassure them if possible. It may be hard to do so, however. Although confidentiality is central to counseling, its legal status in a school setting is ambiguous. A professor of social work calls schools "one of the most problematic settings for social workers to work in and maintain 'client' confidentiality."[246]

A North Carolina expert on school social work agrees that, while counselors' academic preparation usually emphasizes confidentiality, they may find a different reality in practice. From practicing in schools himself, he recalls people shouting confidential information across crowded halls; an insufficiently private setting for meeting with students or other members of the social work team; occasional breaches of confidentiality by teachers with whom

244. Edwin M. Speas Jr., Senior Deputy Attorney General, Thomas J. Ziko, Special Deputy Attorney General, and Laura C. Crumpler, Assistant Attorney General, to Richard L. Thompson, Deputy State Superintendent, Department of Public Instruction, November 3, 1997.

245. Anne Dellinger, *Parental Rights and School Health: North Carolina Legislation,* 28 SCHOOL LAW BULLETIN 1–9, at 3, 5, 7, and 8 (Chapel Hill, N.C., Institute of Government, Winter 1997).

246. Kopels, Sandra, *Response to 'Confidentiality: A different perspective,'* 15 SOCIAL WORK IN EDUCATION 250–252, at 251 (1993), cited in "Confidentiality and School Social Work: A Practice Perspective," *Children, Families, & Schools,* Washington, D.C.: National Association of Social Workers, Vol. 2, No. 2 (October 2001).

information was shared; and school "sign-in" procedures that asked the counselor who is being seen and why. This expert surmises that counselors who come to doubt the schools' commitment to confidentiality often respond by recording little of what they do. Unfortunately, he adds, inadequate record-keeping conceals the extent and value of counselors' work and, if a serious problem develops, increases the counselor's and LEA's liability exposure.[247]

The legal status of confidentiality is determined by state and federal statutes and regulations and by ethical standards and guidance from professional organizations. North Carolina statutes give "evidentiary privileges" to anyone who confides in a licensed psychologist[248] or school counselor[249] certified by DPI[250] (but not in a school social worker[251]). However, having an evidentiary privilege does not mean that what a student tells a professional must remain between them. It means only that a psychologist or school counselor may not reveal the information *in a judicial proceeding* unless the student permits it or the judge decides that the testimony "is necessary to a proper administration of justice."

The North Carolina Administrative Code requires everyone licensed by the State Board of Education to "keep in confidence personally identifiable information regarding students or their family members that has been obtained in the course of professional service, unless disclosure is required or permitted by law or professional standards, or is necessary for the personal safety of the

247. Telephone conversation with Gary L. Shaffer, Assoc. Professor, School of Social Work, The University of North Carolina at Chapel Hill, April 2, 2003.

248. G.S. 8-53.3.

249. The North Carolina State Board of Education (Policy ID Number QP-A-017) and the North Carolina Administrative Code (16 NCAC 6C.0304) distinguish school counselors from school psychologists and school social workers.

250. G.S. 8-53.4. *See also* G.S. 115C-401.

251. G.S. 8-53.7 provides a privilege to those receiving private social work services, but services rendered in or through a contract with a public school are presumably not private. The school counselor and psychologist privileges cited above do not distinguish between public and private services.

student or others."[252] The Code does not define "safety of the student or others," but there are definitions in state statute that may be useful.[253]

Various other state statutes mention the need for confidentiality of student records. For example,

- Student records are not public records.[254]

- No one contracting with an LEA may sell personally identifiable student information without consent from the student's parent or guardian.[255]

- Principals and other school employees who see juvenile court records about a student must not reveal information in the records. Doing so is grounds for dismissal.[256]

A federal law, the Family Educational Rights and Privacy Act (FERPA), generally requires schools to protect student information, releasing it only with the consent of a parent or the student (if eighteen or older).[257] FERPA lets parents see their minor children's school records, but counselors' personal notes are not considered school records.[258] As a result, although parents may have agreed to the student's counseling, FERPA would not always require that the content of the counseling sessions be shared with them.

Another federal statute strongly guards the confidentiality—even the identity—of anyone in a federally assisted program related to alcohol or drug abuse.[259] Any public school with a program devoted in whole or part

252. 16 NCAC 6C.0602(b)(6).

253. G.S. 122C-3(11); G.S. 90-21.4.

254. G.S. 115C-402(e). Public records are "the property of the people" and anyone "may obtain copies . . . free or at minimal cost unless otherwise specifically provided by law." G.S. 132-1(b).

255. G.S. 115C-401.1.

256. G.S. 115C-404.

257. 20 U.S.C. § 1232g. The regulations are at 34 C.F.R. Part 99.

258. Specifically, records of school staff that "are in the sole possession of the maker thereof and which are not accessible or revealed to any other person except a substitute" are not education records under FERPA. 20 U.S.C. § 1232g(a)(4)(B)(i).

259. 42 U.S.C. § 290dd-2. Regulations are at 42 C.F.R. Part 2.

to substance abuse treatment (including merely counseling) is covered by the law.[260] However, school programs and activities that are purely educational are not covered. The statute is complicated: For example, important matters that are beyond the scope of this guide include what a covered program may disclose, with whose consent, and how the federal law fits with North Carolina law[261] on minors' consent, with a therapist's "duty to warn,"[262] and with FERPA.[263] Counselors who think the law may cover their activities should consult the LEA's attorney. A helpful publication for an attorney is *Handbook: Legal Issues for School-Based Programs* (2d ed., 1996), published by the Legal Action Center of the City of New York.

Finally, a number of national organizations for counselors advise keeping a student's confidence unless there is a greater obligation to breach it. In North Carolina the State Board of Education reinforces the advice by requiring counselors to adhere to their profession's standards and codes.[264] Counseling organizations with statements on confidentiality include the American School Counselor Association,[265] School Social Work Association

---

260. A covered program is one where a certified professional assesses, diagnoses, treats, or refers students for substance abuse problems. 42 U.S.C. § 290dd-2(a) and 42 C.F.R. § 2.11.

261. 42 C.F.R. § 2.20 preserves only state laws that offer greater confidentiality.

262. Unlike most other states, North Carolina has not yet recognized a therapist's duty to warn someone the patient may harm as a separate legal duty—separate, that is, from the general duty not to act negligently. Gregory v. Kilbride, 150 N.C. App. 601, 565 S.E.2d 685 (2002).

263. The U.S. Department of Education, which enforces FERPA, and the Alcohol, Drug Abuse and Mental Health Administration, a division of the U.S. Department of Health and Human Services, acknowledged in 1990 in a joint opinion letter that the two laws are partially contradictory.

264. See Policy ID Number QP-F-008, "Policy delineating the job description and performance criteria for School Counselors," *North Carolina State Board of Education Policy Manual;* Policy ID Number QP-F-009, "Policy delineating the job description and performance criteria for the School Social Worker," *id.;* and "Policy ID Number QP-F-006, Policy delineating the job description and performance criteria for student services personnel," *id.*

265. A.2 and B.2, *Ethical Standards for School Counselors* (June 25, 1998), available at http://www.schoolcounselor.org.

of America,[266] the National Association of School Psychologists[267] and the National Association of Social Workers.[268] The statements are summarized below.

- American School Counselor Association: Each person has a right to privacy and to expect the counseling relationship to comply with laws, policies, and ethical standards. The counselor should explain how much confidentiality to expect and give the student a written statement about when disclosures may be made.

- School Social Work Association of America: Confidentiality is a core value of social work and is essential to its practice. Social work in schools requires balancing legal and ethical duties. Practitioners must know and obey the law and school policies and tell students and families, before rendering services, when confidentiality might be breached. Information should be shared with other school personnel only for compelling professional reasons and "the focus should always be on what is best for the student." Social workers have a duty to warn (breach confidentiality) about a clear and present danger to the student or another identifiable person.

- National Association of School Psychologists: Clients should be told the limits of confidentiality. "Information is revealed only with the informed consent of the client, or the client's parent or legal guardian, except in those situations in which failure to release information would result in clear danger to the client or others." Psychologists share information only for

266. *Position Statement: School Social Workers and Confidentiality* (March 15, 2001), available at http://www.sswaa.org.

267. See especially III.A9 and III.C2, *Principles for Professional Ethics* (1997 ed.) and *Professional Conduct Manual for School Psychology* (Bethesda, M.D.: National Association of School Psychologists 2002), at 19–21.

268. *NASW Standards for School Social Work Services* (June 2002); NASW Commission on Education, *Position Statement: The School Social Worker and Confidentiality*; and *Confidentiality and School Social Work: A Practice Perspective*, Washington, D.C.: National Association of Social Workers (October 2001).

professional reasons and only with those who need to know. Parents' consent is sought before treating a student on an on-going basis. Parents are notified as soon as possible if a student who cannot legally consent to treatment on his own seeks treatment. Findings and progress are reported frankly and promptly to parents.

- National Association of Social Workers: School social workers must comply with legislation, regulations, and school policies on confidentiality. The uses of information should be dictated by best practice and ethical and legal considerations. The psychologist should inform all parties of confidentiality limits and requirements when starting treatment. The LEA should provide the social worker and community–school team members with work resources to assure privacy and confidentiality. The position statement of the National Association of Social Workers' Commission on Education defines terms, describes relevant law, and advises on practice. A practice update on confidentiality and school social work observes that social workers cannot serve students without sharing information about them. The difficulty is in knowing what to share with whom. The update urges sharing only information with educational relevance, that which advances the academic success or social, emotional, or mental well-being of the student. It also notes the principal exceptions to confidentiality: reporting child maltreatment or a student's dangerous intent. (Most of the other organizations mention these exceptions as well.)

Although professional organizations recognize a legal and ethical duty to preserve some confidentiality in school counseling, as a practical matter they do not explain how a counselor should proceed. A counselor will benefit from knowing the LEA's policy and state law before drawing on his or her own judgment.

REPORTING SUSPICION OF DEPENDENCY
OR A CARETAKER'S ABUSE OR NEGLECT

Everyone in North Carolina is legally responsible for protecting children[269] from mistreatment by parents, guardians, custodians,[270] or caretakers.[271] Any person or institution with a reasonable suspicion that a child is abused, neglected, or dependent must report it to the local Department of Social Services (DSS).[272] Since school personnel are well situated to observe children, the duty very often falls on them. North Carolina law refers to the reporting obligation[273] and the state School Boards Association has a model policy explaining the need to report and cooperate with DSS investigations.[274] The law protects school personnel who report reasonable suspicions even if they are mistaken.[275] The state court of appeals has applied the statute to protect a principal and his school system from liability.[276] The principal had reported students' allegations of abuse to DSS and to an assistant superintendent and to no one else. The court found both the reports justified despite the fact that the person who was reported was acquitted of criminal charges.

269. A child is anyone under eighteen years of age and not married, emancipated, or a member of the armed forces of the United States. G.S. 7B-101(14).

270. The "person or agency . . . awarded legal custody of a juvenile by a court or a person . . . who has assumed the status and obligation of a parent without being awarded . . . legal custody. . . ." G.S. 7B-101(8).

271. "Any person other than a parent, guardian, or custodian who has responsibility for the health and welfare of a juvenile in a residential setting." "Caretaker" includes a stepparent, a foster parent, an adult member of the child's household, a relative caring for a child, staff in residential child care facilities, or employees or volunteers in facilities operated by the N.C. Department of Health and Human Services. G.S. 7B-101(3).

272. G.S. 7B-301, and *see generally* Ch. 7B, Subchapter 1.

273. G.S. 115C-400.

274. NCSBA, Policy 4240, Child Abuse—Reports and Investigations, Policies to Lead the Schools, Raleigh, N.C.

275. G.S. 7B-309.

276. Davis v. Durham City Schools, 91 N.C. App. 520, 372 S.E.2d 318 (1988), applying former G.S. 7A-550.

Frequently, the school board has a policy requiring staff to report possible mistreatment to a school official—the principal, perhaps, or the superintendent. Such a policy can be useful, for example, in maintaining the school system's awareness that more than one report has been made or was considered about a particular child over a period of months or years. However, it is essential that anyone who reasonably suspects mistreatment understand that his or her legal duty is to report to DSS. Informing a school official of concern about a child or an intention to report *does not* fulfill that duty. Any policy that requires school personnel to report to someone other than a DSS worker—someone who then decides whether to authorize a report—violates state law.

As noted above, school counselors and psychologists have state statutory "privileges" protecting student confidences to some degree,[277] but the privileges do not excuse these individuals from reporting suspected abuse, neglect, or dependency to DSS or testifying about it.[278]

The law does not require that all harm to minors be reported. Only dependency and abuse or neglect committed by people caring for a child must be reported. If someone suspects that a student is being harmed but does not know who is responsible or what the person's relationship to the student is, a report should certainly be made. DSS will investigate and, if the harm is coming from a non-caretaker, will inform law enforcement. There is a very useful publication on this subject: Janet Mason's *Reporting Child Abuse and Neglect in North Carolina* (2d ed.).[279] It explains essential terms, describes the reporting process and its possible resolutions, and offers helpful advice. Mason emphasizes, *"If in doubt, make the report."*[280]

---

277. The counselors' privilege is found in G.S. 8-53.4. The psychologists' privilege is similar but is not "grounds for excluding evidence . . . of an illness of or injuries to a child. . . ." G.S. 8-53.3. Each states that a judge may waive the privilege when "in his opinion disclosure is necessary to a proper administration of justice."

278. G.S. 7B-310.

279. JANET MASON, REPORTING CHILD ABUSE AND NEGLECT IN NORTH CARLOLINA (Chapel Hill, N.C., Institute of Government 2003).

280. *Id.* at 45.

The first three conditions described below—abuse, neglect, and dependency —must be reported to DSS. The remainder of the section describes other troubling situations and the choices open to adults who observe them.

Parents[281] are abusive if they inflict serious physical injury on a child or treat a child in a way that produces serious emotional damage. They are also being abusive if they create or allow a risk of serious physical injury. Using cruel or grossly inappropriate discipline is abuse,[282] and so is condoning a child's delinquent acts.[283]

Some definitions of abuse are particularly relevant to pregnant and parenting adolescents. Sexual involvement between a minor and a caretaker is abuse, as are certain serious sex-related acts that a parent permits or encourages, including "taking indecent liberties with a child," regardless of the age of the parties.[284] Thus, a parent who allows or encourages a child under eighteen to engage in criminal sexual activity with a person of any age is abusive. Other acts that qualify as abuse are first- and second-degree rape, sexual offense, or sexual exploitation; incest; and involvement with pornography and obscenity.

Often parents are unaware of an adolescent's sexual activity or, if they know, cannot control it. However, if they are indifferent or seem to approve of it, they could be considered either abusive (see above) or neglectful. Neglect includes a parent's lack of "care, supervision, or discipline" or allowing a child to live in a harmful environment.[285] Thus, a parent who allows a child's partner to live in the family home[286] or the minor to live out of the home with the partner might fit both the abuse and neglect definitions.

281. "Parents" should be understood to mean also guardians, custodians, and caretakers.
282. G.S. 7B-101(1)c.
283. G.S. 7B-101(1)f.
284. G.S. 7B-101(1)d.
285. G.S. 7B-101(15).
286. The medical records that Arlene M. Davis reviewed of girls pregnant under age fifteen contained several instances.

When a young woman has no parent, or none able to care for her, and no appropriate alternative arrangement, the North Carolina juvenile code calls her "dependent."[287] Pregnant or parenting minors can become dependent in a number of circumstances. A significant number of homeless girls are pregnant. They may have left home because of the pregnancy or become pregnant on the street, where young people are often sexually exploited.[288]

These girls are also overrepresented among runaways.[289] State law calls runaway youth "undisciplined,"[290] but an individual youngster can be hard to categorize. While some runaways abandon a safe home, others leave as a result of abuse, neglect, dependency—or a combination. As the U.S. Department of Justice notes, "Runaways can be distinguished from throwaways in theory, but distinguishing between them in practice is very difficult because many episodes of both result from some sort of family conflict."[291]

A third group who may become dependent are young women who have entered the United States unaccompanied by a parent and perhaps without a parent's knowledge or approval. Some observers report that the number of such youngsters is increasing.[292]

287. G.S. 7B-101(9).

288. Telephone conversation with Julie Bosland, Special Assistant to the Commissioner, Administration on Children, Youth and Families, U.S. Department of Health and Human Services, February 2, 2000.

289. *Id.*

290. G.S. 7B-1501(27).

291. Louise Hanson, *Second Comprehensive Study of Missing Children,* OJJDP JUVENILE JUSTICE BULLETIN 179085 (April 2000), at 3. Available at www.ncjrs.org.

292. An American Bar Association listserv for people involved with child welfare issues posted this inquiry, "How is your jurisdiction responding to unaccompanied minors who travel to this country from Central or South America?" The questioner, located in Virginia, described "a large number of minor girls . . . without a parent or guardian . . . with their boyfriends . . . over the age of 21. Some of these young women become victims of domestic violence while others become pregnant." Inquiry posted September 20, 2000, at CHILDCASE@MAIL.ABANET.ORG.

NON-CARETAKERS HARMING STUDENTS

State law requires principals to inform law enforcement when certain crimes are committed on school property.[293] Otherwise, whether to report harm by non-caretakers can be a difficult decision. At a minimum, whenever a student is thought to have been harmed, the school must try to learn whether the perpetrator is or is not a caretaker.

Two problem areas for adolescents, about which schools should be concerned, are sexual assault and domestic violence. These are harms to which a significant number of teens, especially the youngest, are exposed.[294] The behaviors can overlap: for example, sexually assaulting a person with whom one has or has had a personal relationship is also domestic violence. Furthermore, some acts of domestic violence or sexual assault also meet the definition of child abuse—and thus have to be reported to DSS. Usually, however, someone not related to the victim commits domestic violence and sexual assaults. In that case, school employees must look to school policy, professional standards, advice from colleagues or superiors, and their own best judgment for guidance in how to protect the student and whether and to whom to report the incident. FERPA should also be considered before informing anyone other than parents. Reporting to an outside agency or individual, such as law enforcement, would not violate FERPA if no education record were made of it. Alternatively, the school might conclude that a report was permitted under FERPA's emergency exception.

293. The crimes are assault resulting in serious personal injury, sexual assault, sexual offense, rape, kidnapping, indecent liberties with a minor, various weapons offenses, and unlawful possession of a controlled substance. G.S. 115C-288(g).

294. In the 1995 National Survey of Family Growth, thirteen percent of fifteen- to nineteen-year-olds who had had sex said they had been forced. Twenty-two percent of fifteen- to forty-four-year-old women who began sex before age fifteen said the sex was involuntary. Debra Kalmuss et al., *Preventing Sexual Risk Behaviors and Pregnancy Among Teenagers: Linking Research and Programs,* 35 PERSPECTIVES ON SEXUAL AND REPRODUCTIVE HEALTH 87–93 (March/April 2003). Available at http://www.agi-usa.org.

Domestic Violence

Although readers may think of domestic violence as a problem of mature women, that is not the case. Pregnant or parenting adolescents are at substantial risk of domestic violence. Women in the United States report partner assaults in alarming numbers,[295] and far more violence is thought to occur than is reported.[296] Moreover, the danger is greater to adolescent[297] or pregnant[298] women than to women in general. If a pregnant woman is abused, there is also a possibility of harm to her pregnancy[299] and to infants and young children. About half of men who abuse partners also abuse children living in the home.[300]

295. For example, 54 percent of women seen in one emergency room said they had been threatened or injured by an intimate partner sometime during their lives. J. Abbott, et al., *Domestic Violence Against Women: Incidence and prevalence in an emergency department population,* 273 JAMA 1763–1767 (June 14, 1995).

Men also suffer domestic violence, but researchers conclude, based on frequency, severity, and fear of injury, that "intimate partner violence should be considered first and foremost a crime against women." Patricia Tjaden and Nancy Thoennes, *Extent, Nature, and Consequences of Intimate Partner Violence,* NCJ 181867, Washington, D.C.: U.S. Department of Justice (July 2000), at 55.

In North Carolina 34,902 women and 2,113 men called a crisis center in a year to report abuse. Report of the North Carolina Council for Women's Domestic Violence Program, July 1, 1999–June 30, 2000.

296. *Violence,* Position Paper of the American Academy of Family Physicians (2000), at 1. Available at www.aafp.org.

297. Constance M. Weimann et al., *Pregnant Adolescents: Experiences and Behaviors Associated with Physical Assault by an Intimate Partner,* 4 MATERNAL AND CHILD HEALTH J. 93–101(2000); and Barbara Parker et al., *Physical and Emotional Abuse In Pregnancy: A Comparison of Adult and Teenage Women,* 42 NURSING RESEARCH 173–177 (1993).

298. Twenty-six percent of pregnant teens report physical abuse from partners, and 40 to 60 percent, depending on the study, say the abuse began or increased with pregnancy. Nancy Worchester, *A More Hidden Crime: Adolescent Battered Women,* THE NETWORK NEWS, National Women's Health Network (July/Aug. 1993), at 4.

299. March of Dimes Birth Defects Foundation, *Fact Sheet: Domestic Violence & Teenage Pregnancy* (1996).

300. American Psychological Association, *Violence and the Family: report of the APA Presidential Task Force on Violence and the Family,* Washington, D.C. (1996), at 80 (hereafter APA Report).

A North Carolina statute defines domestic violence as any one of the wrongful acts named in the statute committed against a person—or a minor child living with or in the custody of the person—by someone with whom the person has, or did have, a personal relationship.[301] Notice that under the definition the partners need not live together. This is important in the case of adolescents because they very often are not married to or living with their partner and never have. The relationship can be that of current or former spouses, persons of the opposite sex who are living together or have lived together in the past, parent and child or grandparent and grandchild,[302] persons who have a child in common, or current or former members of the same household; or it may be a current or former dating relationship between members of the opposite sex.[303]

A young woman who suffers domestic violence may benefit from a civil protective order.[304] The order lets a judge act in various ways to protect her. Besides directing the abuser to stop and leave her alone in the future, a judge can regulate the couple's housing, child custody and support, and personal property and require the abuser to pay legal costs and attorney fees and even to accept treatment.[305] Violating a civil protective order is a crime.[306] Evidence and opinion are divided on when and for what kinds of victims orders are most helpful.[307] A victim should be told all her options and informed that an order may offer protection, albeit limited protection.

301. G.S. 50B-1.

302. Or it may be a similar relationship, "acting in loco parentis to a minor child." A child of any age may be the victim, but a child must be sixteen or older to be considered the abuser. G.S. 50B-1(b).

303. *Id.*

304. G.S. 50B-2 through -4.2.

305. G.S. 50B-3.

306. G.S. 50B-4.1.

307. In one study, six months after obtaining an order, 65 percent of victims had had no further problem. ABA Domestic Violence statistics, available at www.abanet, citing *CPOs: the Benefits and Limitations for Victims of Domestic Violence,* National Center for State Courts Research Report (1997).

She can seek a protective order by going to the office of the clerk of superior court in a county courthouse and asking for the forms,[308] which are also available on the Internet.[309] If she is under eighteen she must bring an adult friend or relative to serve as her guardian ad litem (GAL).[310] If she cannot pay the court costs she may file as an indigent.[311] She does not have to have a lawyer,[312] although it might be to her advantage.[313] If she has no lawyer, the GAL files the necessary forms, which are available in Spanish and English. After the alleged abuser is notified, the minor will be granted an emergency hearing, usually within ten days. The GAL may even ask that an order be granted immediately, before the alleged abuser is notified.[314]

Law enforcement officers can help, too. A domestic violence victim can "request the assistance of a local law enforcement agency . . . [which] shall respond as soon as practicable."[315] An officer can take steps to protect her and tell her where to find shelter, medical care, counseling, and other services. If "feasible," the officer will take her to appropriate facilities for care

308. G.S. 50B-2(a) and (d).

309. First, enter http://www.nccourts.org. Under the page heading, The North Carolina Court System, click Judicial Forms. Next, enter AOC-CV-303 in the first box and click Search.

310. G.S. 1A-1, Rule 17(b). If the defendant (the alleged abuser) is a minor, a GAL must also be appointed for him. The form for the appointment of a GAL in domestic violence actions is AOC-CV-318.

There are several kinds of guardians ad litem. All are appointed to represent a minor's best interest in a particular case. The AOC Guardian Ad Litem Program provides GALs for abuse, neglect, or dependency proceedings. GALs for other proceedings are appointed under Rule 17 or other statutes.

311. G.S. 1-110.

312. G.S. 50B-2(a). Joan Brannon, *Domestic Violence in North Carolina*, unpublished manuscript, Institute of Government (October 2000). No one bringing a civil lawsuit in North Carolina is entitled to a court-appointed attorney. See G.S. 7A-451 for cases in which the state provides counsel. A Legal Services attorney might assist the adolescent in some counties.

313. Orloff, Leslye E. et al., *With No Place to Turn: Improving Legal Advocacy for Battered Immigrant Women*, 29 Family Law Quarterly 313–329, at 319 (Summer 1995).

314. G.S. 50B-2(b).

315. G.S. 50B-5(a).

and to her home to remove needed items.[316] If an officer declines to help her retrieve personal belongings, she can seek that assistance as part of a protective order.[317]

A violent act against a partner is often a crime as well as a civil injury, allowing the victim to seek help in criminal court, too. Acts of domestic violence that are also crimes include assaults, battery, rape, and other sexual offenses.[318] Stalking, communicating threats, or destruction of property might also qualify.

Adults can help a young woman experiencing domestic violence by explaining her legal remedies to her and referring her to private agencies. A domestic violence hotline is an important resource for many victims, and one that adolescents are especially likely to use. Professionals should know that a victim need not be planning to leave a partner in order to call or use the services of a domestic violence program. Many victims seek help a number of times, as a first or an interim step, before they leave an abuser.[319] The National Domestic Violence Hotline (1-800-799-SAFE [7233]) can refer callers to a local program or shelter. During normal business hours the North Carolina Coalition Against Domestic Violence also refers callers to local programs.[320]

316. *Id.*

317. Joan Brannon, *Magistrate's Role in Domestic Violence Protective Orders,* Institute of Government (January 2001), 120.

318. "(1) Attempting to cause bodily injury, or intentionally causing bodily injury; or (2) Placing the aggrieved party or a member of the aggrieved party's family or household in fear of imminent serious bodily injury or continued harassment, as defined in G.S. 14-277.3, that rises to such a level as to inflict substantial emotional distress; or (3) Committing any act defined in G.S. 14-27.2 through G.S. 14-27.7" [*i.e.,* first- and second-degree rape, first- and second-degree sexual offense, and intercourse and sexual offenses with certain victims (children in a home where the defendant "has assumed the position of a parent" or students where the defendant is a school staff member)]. G.S. 50B-1.

319. "Many women do return to the abuser many times during the process of ending the abuse." APA Report, at 66.

320. Unless otherwise attributed, the information in this paragraph is from Marie French, training specialist, North Carolina Coalition Against Domestic Violence, December 12, 2000. The Coalition is located in Durham and can be reached at (919) 956-9124.

Most local programs in North Carolina offer twenty-four hour hotlines, advocacy in court, support groups, and shelter for victims. The programs differ, however, and adults advising a student should learn what services are offered locally. Most shelters accept minors on an emergency basis and work with them to normalize their legal status.

Sexual Assault

When teachers, counselors, school nurses, and other advisers counsel a pregnant or parenting adolescent they should consider the possibility that the student has been sexually assaulted. There is considerable evidence that pre- and early-teen sexual activity is often involuntary.[321] A young female frequently has less power and experience than her partner and in some instances will have been directly coerced. A substantial age difference "may make it hard for the young woman to resist [a partner's] approaches and even more difficult for her to insist that contraceptives be used to prevent STDs and pregnancy."[322] Judith Musick, a teen pregnancy researcher who also works with teen mothers, states that while girls may appear to be eager initiators of sex, this "is probably not the case for many girls who become mothers in their teens, and it is surely not the case for those who become pregnant in their very early teens."[323]

---

321. Teens report rape and other sexual assaults at a higher rate than any other age group. Forty-four percent of victims in the rapes reported to police are girls under eighteen. Two-thirds of imprisoned rapists and sex offenders report having victims under eighteen and 58 percent say they had a victim twelve or younger. Lawrence A. Greenfeld, *Sex Offenses and Offenders: An Analysis of Data on Rape and Sexual Assault*, NCJ 163392, U.S. Department of Justice (February 1997). Available at www.ojp.usdoj.gov/bjs.

322. ALAN GUTTMACHER INSTITUTE, SEX AND AMERICA'S TEENAGERS 74 (1994). *See also* David J. Landry & Jacqueline Darroch Forrest, *How Old Are U.S. Fathers?* 27 FAM. PLAN. PERSP. 159, 165 (1995). For a general discussion of the legal context, see SHARON ELSTEIN & NOY DAVIS, ABA CTR. ON CHILDREN AND THE LAW, SEXUAL RELATIONSHIPS BETWEEN ADULT MALES AND YOUNG TEEN GIRLS: EXPLORNG THE LEGAL AND SOCIAL RESPONSES (1997).

323. JUDITH MUSICK, YOUNG, POOR, AND PREGNANT: THE PSYCHOLOGY OF TEENAGE MOTHERHOOD 74 (1993).

One study found that 61 percent of teen mothers reported at least one coercive sexual experience. Almost 30 percent of those reporting coercion said it was by a family member; more than 50 percent, by a male friend. Of the males involved in the study, 46 percent were more than ten years older than their partners.[324] In a sample of North Carolina girls pregnant before age fifteen, 10 of 186 girls reported when they sought medical care that they had been raped.[325] Coercion was almost certainly more common than that number indicates, since the health providers often had not recorded the patients' age at first intercourse, the number and age of partners, or other sexual history that might have led to discussion of coercive experiences.[326]

School personnel should know that the following acts are criminal in North Carolina:

- Vaginal intercourse is defined as first-degree rape when one partner is twelve years old or younger and the other is at least twelve years old and at least four years older than the other partner.[327]

- Other sex acts (for example, fellatio, anal intercourse, and cunnilingus) are first-degree sexual offenses when one partner is twelve or younger and the other is at least twelve and four or more years older.[328]

- If one partner is thirteen, fourteen, or fifteen and the other is more than four years older, vaginal intercourse is statutory

324. Harold P. Gershon et al., *The Prevalence of Coercive Sexual Experience among Teenage Mothers*, 4 J. INTERPERSONAL VIOLENCE 204 (June 1989).

325. Arlene M. Davis, codirector of the Adolescent Pregnancy Project, reviewed these records between April 1996 and December 1998. See the Preface for a fuller description of them.

326. Of the 186 records, 133 did not list the girl's age at first intercourse; 134 did not state how many partners she had had; 101 did not state the age of the FOP (father of the pregnancy). When father's age was given, it was eighteen or older more than half the time.

327. G.S. 14-27.2.

328. G.S. 14-27.4(a).

rape,[329] unless they are "lawfully married." The penalties are greater if the older partner is six or more years older.[330]

- Intercourse "by force and against the will" of one partner, no matter what the partners' ages, is second-degree rape.[331] The force need not be physical; inducing fear can be enough.[332]

- Regardless of age, incest between grandparent and grand-child; parent and child or stepchild; or brother and sister is a felony,[333] as is an adult's intercourse with a minor residing in a home where the adult has the position of a parent.[334]

Some prosecutors and law enforcement agencies hesitated at first to enforce the statutory rape law,[335] but that has changed even when the perpetrator is a teen himself.[336] In 2002, 1,366 statutory rape charges were brought in district court in North Carolina.[337] The federal Welfare Reform Act encourages prosecution of statutory rape and requires states to educate law enforcement and other agencies about it.[338]

---

329. The North Carolina statute uses "statutory rape" to designate intercourse between thirteen-, fourteen-, and fifteen-year-olds and significantly older partners, regardless of whether the younger party consents. State v. Anthony, 351 N.C. 611, 528 S.E.2d 321 (2000). Many in law enforcement, however, use the term for any rape or sexual offense to which the victim's consent is not a defense.

330. G.S. 14-27.7A.

331. G.S. 14-27.3.

332. State v. Martin, 126 N.C. App. 426, 485 S.E.2d 352 (1997).

333. G.S. 14-178.

334. G.S. 14-27.7. As noted, this is also child abuse.

335. *No Convictions under Tougher Statutory Rape Law,* THE NEWS & OBSERVER (Raleigh, N.C), Nov. 26, 1997, at 3A. *See, e.g., 11-year-old Chatham Girl Missing,* THE NEWS & OBSERVER (Raleigh, N.C.), Dec. 24, 1998, at 6B.

336. *Statutory rape charge filed against 19-year-old,* THE NEWS & OBSERVER (Raleigh, N.C.), Nov. 1, 2001, at 3B.

337. Telephone conversation with Patrick Tamer, Statistician, North Carolina Administrative Office of the Courts, June 3, 2003.

338. 42 U.S.C. § 602(a)(1)(A)(vi). However, few states seem to have implemented the directive. Jodie Levin-Epstein, *State TANF Plans: Out-of-Wedlock and Statutory Rape Provisions,* Washington, D.C.: Center for Law and Social Policy (1997), at 4–6. Available at www.clasp.org.

ENCOURAGING SCHOOL COMPLETION

The stakes in a pregnant or parenting girl's decision about leaving school are very high. Helping her stay and graduate is the greatest contribution school boards and personnel make to her life and her children's. The Alan Guttmacher Institute said about the connection between teen pregnancies, parenting, and educational achievement:

> [D]ropping out of school, not having a baby, is the key factor that sets adolescent mothers behind their peers. If a pregnant teenager does drop out, it is unlikely that she will return to school before her children are in school. Adolescent mothers who stay in school are almost as likely eventually to graduate (73 percent) as women who do not become mothers while in high school (77 percent). In contrast, only about 30 percent of women who drop out of high school either before or after their baby's birth eventually graduates.[339] (citations omitted)

Some young people are "pushed out" of schools—told they are "over-age" or not making satisfactory progress and therefore must leave—and most of them do not know they have a legal right to stay. New York City school officials, including the Chancellor, acknowledged that the practice has taken hold there and said they will try to halt it.[340] The New York Times reported, "In interviews with dozens of discharged students from all over the city, only one student had heard that she had a legal right to attend school until twenty-one—and that was because she overheard her attendance officer trying unsuccessfully to argue the point with the guidance counselor who said she had to leave the school."[341] School officials in Houston allegedly encouraged students to leave and altered records to conceal the actual dropout

339. ALAN GUTTMACHER INSTITUTE, SEX AND AMERICA'S TEENAGERS 59 (1994).
340. Tamar Lewin and Jennifer Medina, *To Cut Failure Rate School Shed Students*, NEW YORK TIMES, July 31, 2003, A1, Col. 2–4.
341. *Id.*

rate.[342] These scandals are reminders to administrators, counselors, and teachers—anyone working with North Carolina students who may need more time to graduate—to explain to students and their families that state law lets them stay in school until age twenty-one.[343]

School systems and educators trying hard to keep pregnant and parenting students enrolled have problems, including lack of information. In 1981 the Rand Corporation wrote:

> How many students are mothers and how many stay in school is
> a matter of opinion rather than fact in most districts. Most LEAs
> keep no statistics on dropouts by reason for termination; in the
> few LEAs that keep such figures most respondents, including
> those responsible for collecting them, doubt their validity. Formal
> records of pregnancies are not kept anywhere. In the absence of
> valid data, school staff opinions vary wildly: Estimates of the per-
> centage of pregnant students and teenage mothers remaining in
> school ranged from 10 percent to 90 percent in one district.[344]

Not knowing who leaves school, or why, or whether those persons even-tually complete secondary education remains a serious problem nationally and for our state. While North Carolina has had no scandals, its dropout data has been sharply criticized by the Education Trust.[345] Certainly, it is in-adequate. The General Assembly has recognized the fact[346] and asked the

342. Zanto Peabody, *Audit confirms HISD's procedure to count dropouts is in disarray*, HOUSTON CHRONICLE, April 11, 2003; *Teachers to keep tabs on potential dropouts by computer*, HOUSTON CHRONICLE, July 30, 2003; Diana Jean Schemo, *Questions on Data Cloud Luster of Houston Schools*, NEW YORK TIMES, July 10, 2003.

343. G.S. 115C-1; 115C-366(a).

344. Rand Corporation Report at 85.

345. *Telling the Whole Truth (or Not) about High School Graduation*, Washington, D.C.: The Education Trust (2003).

346. N.C. 2003 Session Laws, House Joint Resolution 1137, "Authorizing the Legislative Research Commission to Study Issues Related to Data Collection by the Department of Public Instruction."

State Board of Education to improve the data.[347] The State Board has agreed to do so.[348]

Currently, DPI requires each school system and charter school to report dropouts annually but does not check for accuracy.[349] The department no longer requires LEAs to say how many school-age pregnant girls live in the district or how many of them the schools are serving as children with special needs.[350] Most importantly, DPI requires the student leaving school or the person in each LEA who reports dropout events to choose *one* reason from a list for why the student is leaving school. Pregnancy, though not parenting (which probably causes more withdrawals), is one of the reasons on the list.[351]

The problem with this process is that at least thirteen of the twenty-one reasons from which the student or reporter must choose might easily fit the circumstances of a pregnant or parenting student.[352] How could such a student

347. S. L. 2002-178, amending G.S. 115C-12.

348. The State Board has said that in 2003–2004 it will "[r]evamp dropout reason codes to better capture the conditions and causes leading to students' dropping out of school." *Report to the Joint Legislative Education Oversight Committee*, December 2002, at 4.

349. Instead, DPI makes the LEA's dropout prevention coordinator and superintendent jointly responsible. N.C. Department of Public Instruction, *Dropout Data Report 2001–02*, note at 8.

350. Telephone conversation with Brenda Gilchrist, Division of Exceptional Children, N.C. Department of Public Instruction, September 12, 2002.

351. The reasons are suspected substance abuse; academic problems; attendance family; attendance personal; attendance school; attendance; attendance work; need to care for children; enrollment in a community college; discipline problem; employment necessary; expulsion (permanent); health problems; unstable home environment; incarcerated in adult facility; failure to return after a long-term suspension (11 to 365 days); marriage; moved, school status unknown; pregnancy; runaway; choice of work over school. N.C. DPI, "Withdrawal and Reason Codes," *Dropout Data Collecting and Reporting Procedures Manual 2002*. Available at http://www.ncpublicschools.org.

352. DPI asks that the student select the reason whenever possible. N.C. DPI, "Why Students Drop Out," *Dropout Data Report 2000–01. See also* Policy ID Number HSP-Q-000, *North Carolina State Board of Education Policy Manual*, concerning exit interviews with students dropping out. Both documents are available at http://www.ncpublicschools.org.

choose among, for example, "need to care for children," "employment necessary," and "choice of work over school" as reasons for dropping out? And the remaining reasons—poor attendance, discipline or health problems, substance abuse, running away—can apply to any student, thus concealing how many of those who choose them also have a problem arising from pregnancy or parenting.

As a result of the flawed reporting system, North Carolina records a mere 1 percent of dropout events as due to pregnancy and none to parenting. School officials, policymakers, and the public do not know how many students leave in whole or in part for these reasons.[353] Robeson County provided a dramatic example several years ago. The county's pregnancy rate for fifteen- to seventeen-year-olds was far above the state average,[354] but the school system recorded only two students leaving because of pregnancy in 1996–97, four in 1997–98, and eleven in 1998–99. Robeson school officials recognized the gap in their information, explaining to ACLU-NC:

> **These numbers are taken from our Annual Dropout Count submitted to our State Department of Public Instruction. We acknowledge that these numbers are low. However, due to the dropout codes given by our state (academics, attendance, preg-**

353. When the author first asked DPI how many girls drop out due to pregnancy, the reply was 1.3 percent. But after a short pause the DPI representative added, "Not that I believe that." Telephone conversation with Sylvia Massey, Section Chief, Effective Practice, September 18, 1998.

The problem of North Carolina's imprecise dropout data affects the count of all types of students. With respect to pregnant and parenting students, in 2002 DPI reported that 54 percent of dropout events were due to one of the five attendance reasons (see footnote 351, above). Yet in most cases attendance problems cannot be separated from other reasons—for example, academic problems, which are listed as the reason for only 10 percent of dropouts. N.C. DPI, "Why Students Drop Out," *Dropout Data Report 2002–03,* at 13. Available at http://www.ncpublic schools.org.

354. The state average is 49.4 pregnancies per thousand females fifteen to seventeen years of age in North Carolina. It is 77.4 in Robeson County. State Center for Health Statistics, Division of Public Health, N.C. Department of Health and Human Services, *North Carolina Reported Pregnancies: 1999,* 2-9 and 2-10.

nancy, etc.), we feel that more dropouts (pregnant girls) **actually
left school before graduation than our numbers reflect. They
probably were coded by our schools as 'academics' and 'attendance' reasons for dropping out of school which are obvious
effects that can be associated with pregnancy.**[355]

Although parenting is not officially recognized as a reason for dropping
out, it certainly causes some students to leave school and contributes to others' decisions.[356] Schools' efforts are sometimes focused on pregnant students, only to be withdrawn when they give birth and return to the regular
classroom.[357] New parents face immediate, pressing needs—above all, for
child care and additional income. Parenting responsibilities can affect attendance, which may lead to academic problems and eventually to dropping
out. The State Board excuses absences for a student's own illness but not for
tending to a sick child.

Some students might continue their education if they could transfer with
little interruption to community college, which allows greater flexibility for
scheduling class work, child care, and often employment as well.[358] Local
boards of education are legally required to refer students who are dropping
out to appropriate services including community college,[359] and older secondary school students have a right to transfer there.[360] There are two ways
for a sixteen- or seventeen-year-old to enter community college to finish high
school:

355. Letter responding to a survey from ACLU-NC, August 31, 2000, in
author's files.

356. *See, e.g., Counselor/Advocates: Keeping Pregnant & Parenting Teens in
School,* Alexandria, Virginia: National Association of State Boards of Education
(1990).

357. Rand Corporation Report at 79.

358. Several North Carolinians who work closely with pregnant and parenting
adolescents have expressed this view to the author. For example, interview with
G. Earl Marett, Director, Johnston County Department of Social Services, October
17, 2000.

359. G.S. 115C-47(32).

360. 23 NCAC 2C.0305, Education Services for Minors.

- A student may transfer immediately if her school determines that community college is the best educational option for her and the college permits her to enroll.
- Otherwise, she must stay out of school for six months, after which she has a right to enroll in a community college. At that point she need only submit an application that "is supported by a notarized petition of [her] parent, legal guardian, or other person or agency having legal custody and control."[361]

School employees and others who work with teens are familiar with the second means, but few seem to know about the possibility of immediate transfer, although some students do it every year.[362] The following additional avenues for starting higher education early are open to excellent students:

- The General Assembly is experimenting with allowing intellectually gifted children under sixteen "with the maturity to justify admission" to enroll in community college.[363]
- Another law tells the State Board of Education to see that guidance counselors let ninth graders know they could finish high school in three years; enter four-year colleges early; or, still as high school students, take college courses either at nearby colleges or through distance learning.[364]

School personnel should tell adolescents and their families about all these possibilities. They could also help by encouraging and advocating for an adolescent as she tries to secure the approvals needed to move from school to community college under the first and third methods. At least one LEA is

361. The petition "shall certify the student's residence, date of birth, date of leaving school, and the petitioner's legal relationship to the student." 23 NCAC 2C.0305(b).

362. Fifty-one students transferred in the 2000–2001 school year. Information from Sean Hall, Applications Programmer, Division of Administration, North Carolina Community Colleges System, Raleigh, N.C., December 11, 2001.

363. G.S. 115D-1.1 (expires September 1, 2004).

364. S.L. 2003-251.

experimenting with another plan. The Guilford County schools, in cooperation with two colleges, let students enroll in college to complete high school and begin college work. Two hundred students participated in spring 2002.

In 2003 the General Assembly, at the governor's urging, "set as a priority cooperative efforts between secondary schools and institutions of higher education so as to reduce the high school dropout rate [and] increase high school and college graduation rates. . . ."[365] Boards of community colleges and school boards are encouraged to seek federal, state, local, and private funds to establish joint programs for these purposes. Those at risk of dropping out are the first priority[366] and students are eligible for the programs beginning in ninth grade.[367] The State Board of Education and LEAs are to eliminate policies that discourage students from remaining in school.

IMPROVING SCHOOL POLICIES

When ACLU-NC polled school districts in 2002, it found that about half of the respondents (51 of 104) had a written policy on pregnancy, parenting, or both.[368] Ninety-four offered homebound services and sixty-two allowed pregnant or parenting students to attend an alternative school. ACLU-NC singled out six districts—Asheville, Brunswick, McDowell, Rowan-Salisbury, Rockingham, and Surry—as particularly sensitive to teen parents' needs. On the other hand, the organization expressed concern about

- many districts reporting 0–3 pregnant students in attendance annually;[369]

365. S.L. 2003-277.
366. *Id.* To be codified as G.S. 115C-238.50(a)(1).
367. *Id.* To be codified as G.S. 115C-238.50(f).
368. ACLU-NC sent a first and, if necessary, second letter to the 117 districts, then placed phone calls to many districts. Ultimately, 104 LEAs responded. The results were compiled as *ACLU Pregnant Student Data Chart Analysis February/ March 2002.* Unpublished manuscript; copy in author's files.
369. ACLU staff thought the response indicated that school officials were unaware of pregnant students.

- no response from many districts on the number of dropouts due to pregnancy or parenting;

- some LEAs not providing homebound services to pregnant students;[370]

- more than a third of LEAs (forty) having no standard method of referring students to homebound services or alternative education; and

- half of LEAs *lacking* a written policy on pregnant and parenting students.[371]

The author's review of the responses that LEAs sent to ACLU-NC indicates, first, that some districts' policies are no longer legally permissible and, second, that all LEAs should consider certain issues mentioned below when making policy for these students. The policies described are not identified by LEA.

Homebound Policies

These vary considerably in what services are offered, for how long, when, and under what conditions.[372] The variety may be explained by differences in what LEAs think homebound instruction can accomplish. Some policies caution the student, parent, and physician that homebound instruction is no substitute for being in school and will make passing harder.[373] Others allow

370. LEAs must offer them for the period of medically necessary absence. Section .01501, "Definitions," N, *Procedures Governing Programs and Services for Children with Disabilities* (revised August 3, 2000), at 15. In addition to this requirement of North Carolina law on children with special needs, Title IX requires that a benefit extended to other temporarily disabled students be available to pregnant students.

371. As noted earlier, 16 NCAC 6H.0107(6) and State Board policy (Policy ID Number HSP-D-005) require each LEA to "prepare and implement a written program to meet the special education needs of pregnant students."

372. In practice, differences among LEAs may be smaller than the written policies suggest. The author telephoned the central office of half a dozen school systems to inquire about unusual policies—for example, granting homebound status a month before delivery and saying "students are encouraged to take advantage of this service"—and in each case was told that the policy was no longer, or had never been, implemented as written.

373. For example, one policy cautions, "Homebound/hospital instruction can never replace classroom learning experiences. Normal academic progress cannot be guaranteed."

students two and three months in the homebound program on request. As a legal matter, schools must excuse students for any medical necessity caused by pregnancy, childbirth, miscarriage, abortion, or recovery. The school cannot set a time limit for medically necessary absence. On the other hand, it seems inadvisable and may be discriminatory[374] to encourage students to stay out for prolonged periods. In making policy an LEA should consider legal requirements, how much time at home will benefit a pregnant student, and how much will discourage reentry and school completion.

In some homebound programs staff transfer assignments and completed work between student and teachers, while in others they also instruct the students they visit. The time that a program gives to each student varies from one to six hours a week. Most policies specify the amount of time, but a few say it depends on the student's needs.

Several LEAs rank the conditions that give a student access to homebound instruction. In each policy, the order of priority is (1) accident victims, (2) surgery, (3) extended illnesses, and (4) pregnancy. Some of the policies go further and state that requests for homebound instruction will be considered in this order. If such a policy disadvantages pregnant students it violates both Title IX, which requires that pregnancy be treated like other temporary disabilities, and the state requirement that homebound instruction be provided for children with special needs.

Many policies condition homebound visits on a parent or other adult being present at all times, presumably to protect the student and to keep the LEA and visiting staff member from incurring suspicion or liability. Although there are excellent reasons for the requirement, it must be difficult or impossible for some working families. The apparent strictness on this point among LEAs ranges from "no exceptions will be allowed" (in bold type) to "unless otherwise agreed with the instructor." Some say the adult who is present may be a neighbor, friend, or community volunteer, even "any adult selected by the family."

One policy provides that if the home is unsanitary or unsafe, instruction can be given elsewhere, but the student's parent is responsible for transportation.

374. Two LEAs' policies list "very young age" as a reason for placing a pregnant student on homebound.

In that situation it would seem that, rather than denying homebound instruction, schools should arrange transportation or report possible neglect or dependency to DSS and ask DSS to handle transportation if needed.

Another policy significantly burdens anyone requesting homebound instruction by asking him or her to name a teacher willing to provide it. While it might be reasonable to ask for suggestions, no policy should imply that the student is responsible for identifying an instructor.

Activity Policies

One policy states that school officials may limit a pregnant student's activities if they could endanger her health or that of her fetus. Another forbids contact sports. The legality of these two policies is doubtful. A third, better policy says the school may require a doctor's certificate if the student insists on continuing a possibly hazardous activity.

Attendance Policies

One policy states that "Students who enroll late due to pregnancy will be required to be in attendance 160 days to receive credit for courses." This seems to violate (1) Title IX's general ban on pregnancy discrimination, (2) its specific provision that medically necessary absences must be excused, and (3) the state requirement that pregnant students receive homebound instruction if needed. Another says, "[P]regnant girls can only stay home two weeks after birth, C-section three weeks. They must return to school or they will be counted absent." Again, this policy violates Title IX, which requires excusing absences for medical conditions arising from childbirth or recovery from childbirth. Although an administrator told the author that the school does not enforce the policy against students with medical complications,[375] pregnant students and their families may not know that and may think it useless for the student to return to school after a longer absence.

---

375. Telephone conversation with the LEA's Director of Homebound Services, February 21, 2003.

Assignment/Placement Policies

This category shows the difficulty LEAs face in reconciling Title IX and North Carolina's special education statutes. Half a dozen policies state that the school district's education placement committee decides on a pregnant student's placement, after consulting with the student, family, and perhaps a medical consultant. This is the usual process for children with special needs, but Title IX, on the contrary, allows pregnant students to decide whether to leave their regular program for an alternative. As a federal law Title IX takes precedence over state statute.

Four LEAs share another problematic policy. First, the policy states that pregnant girls may stay in school "within the limits of reasonable safeguards both for the school and the girl. . . ." This conditional statement violates Title IX's guarantee that a pregnant girl may not be excluded from school. Second, the policy states that a "girl's husband . . . and physician should be consulted in developing an educational plan to fit her needs." Since marriage emancipates a minor, there is no reason for school personnel to deal with anyone except a married minor, nor to consult her physician unless that is required for all students with temporary disabilities.

Some pregnant or parenting students are advised to[376] (or ask to) transfer to an alternative school to take advantage of more flexible scheduling or for other reasons. According to state statute, alternative schools are to help students in danger of academic failure (which is often a concern for pregnant or parenting students) and those who exhibit disorderly and disruptive behavior.[377] While these categories may overlap, in most cases they are an uncomfortable pairing. LEAs must think hard about how to meet the needs of pregnant and parenting students (who are usually not behavior problems) when they are in school with others who are referred because of low motivation,

376. Remember that Title IX requires that entering an alternative school, program, or class must be voluntary on the part of a pregnant student. This requirement prohibits a school official's saying, for example, "that is the only place you and your [unborn] baby will be safe" (a comment reported to the author).

377. G.S. 115C-105.45 through -105.48.

underachievement, manipulative behavior, chronic absenteeism, or discipline/ suspension.[378] All students, including those exhibiting the latter behaviors, deserve every opportunity for an education and it may be more difficult for pregnant and parenting students to be well educated in alternative schools. Each of them is entitled to a careful evaluation of needs,[379] a "safe and orderly" school, excellent instruction, and support from school personnel in meeting the challenges presented by early pregnancy and parenting.

OBEYING THE LAW . . . AND DOING MORE

By now the reader understands that a school system—even if following local or state policy—can violate the law through the way counselors, teachers, or administrators treat pregnant and parenting students. This section, addressed primarily to administrators, deals with two topics: complying with the law and exceeding legal requirements in order to improve educational opportunities.

Compliance assessment would likely include these steps:

- Identifying statistical data about the LEA's pregnant and parenting students: For example, how many are enrolled? In what programs and curricula? What is their graduation rate? College enrollment rate? Why do they drop out? Do most affected students and their families think the school has been fair with respect to the issue?

- Trying to assemble important missing data.

- Determining how the middle and high schools actually deal with pregnant and parenting students. For this purpose,

378. One LEA's policy lists these reasons, along with "over-age for grade" and "pregnant and parenting," as justifying placement in an alternative school. The State Board of Education recognizes pregnant students as one kind of "at-risk" student for whom alternative programs may be appropriate. Policy ID Number HSP-Q-001.
379. G.S. 115C-105.48(b).

reviewing written material such as policies and handbooks, and talking to the board and top administrators are important —but not sufficient. It is equally important to ask school nurses, counselors, social workers, and principals. Professionals outside the school system may also have valuable information. Those most likely to be aware of school problems include health department staff or private health providers treating teens, DSS employees, and directors of Adolescent Parenting programs. An investigator might also consult the PTSA or similar groups as well as individual students and their parents.

- Asking the school attorney whether, based on the information above, changes in policy or practice are needed for legal compliance. For example, has the local board adopted written standards for the education of pregnant students? Are they offered homebound instruction when medically necessary? Do any policies or practices discriminate against these students? Is there a Title IX coordinator and do students know his or her identity and that the coordinator handles complaints?

- Training and retraining employees to maintain compliance. Readers may recall (text at Chapter 2, note 10) that when New York Civil Liberties Union interns called public schools to ask whether pregnant women could enroll, "responses varied greatly even within an individual school, depending on who answered the phone." Anyone who has worked in a large organization recognizes the problem. Policies must be clear to everyone allowed to administer them, and higher-level staff has a legal duty to monitor and supervise the implementation.

After achieving legal compliance, an LEA may want to make further efforts to help pregnant students bear healthy babies, if that is their choice, and continue their education. Initiatives within local control would include

- meeting with each pregnant student to assess and try to meet her educational needs;

- allowing greater scheduling flexibility for parenting students;

- cooperating with local colleges to allow immediate transfers;

- allowing school buses to transport students and their children to school daycare centers ; and

- creating an expectation in school personnel, students, families, and advisers that these students, like others, are candidates for the full range of vocational and college opportunities.

Other steps that would benefit these students are beyond LEAs' authority, but local board members and school personnel could be effective advocates. These issues include

- urging DPI to again include pregnant students in the annual "Child Find" count;

- urging the State Board of Education to excuse absences for care of a sick child; and

- urging DPI, first, to ascertain how many North Carolina students leave school due to pregnancy or parenting and, second, to reduce the number.

Issues Associated with Immigrants and Limited-English-Proficient Minors

BY JILL MOORE

A pregnant or parenting minor who is an immigrant poses unique and difficult legal issues. Public school staff may have questions about their legal obligations to their immigrant students. In addition, they may wish to refer an immigrant minor to other public agencies for services. School staff members who could make such referrals should know that immigrant minors are eligible for a number of significant public benefits and services (though not the full range of public benefits and services that are available to their peers who are citizens). Moreover, when an immigrant minor's child is born in the United States, the child is a citizen for purposes of benefit eligibility, irrespective of his parents' immigration status. Finally, minors who have difficulty understanding or speaking English are entitled to receive language assistance from their schools and other public agencies that serve them.

This section introduces some key terms and concepts that pertain to immigrants, their eligibility to attend public school, and their eligibility for other publicly funded benefits and services. It also summarizes public schools' and other public agencies' legal duty to provide language assistance to limited-English-proficient (LEP) persons.

There are many concerns that public schools may have regarding immigrant minors who are pregnant or parenting that could not be addressed here. The adolescent pregnancy project will provide updates and additional information about these issues through its Web site, www.adolescentpregnancy. unc.edu.

WHO IS A CITIZEN? WHO IS AN IMMIGRANT?

People become citizens of the United States either by birth or by a process called "naturalization." Anyone who is born in the U.S., Puerto Rico, the U.S. Virgin Islands, or Guam automatically becomes a citizen at birth.[1] A person born outside the U.S. to a parent who is a U.S. citizen usually becomes a citizen at birth.[2] A person who is born in the "outlying possessions" of the U.S.—American Samoa or Swains Island—is considered a U.S. national, but not a citizen.[3] Some immigrants become citizens of the U.S. by

1. 8 U.S.C. §§ 1401(a), 1401(b), 1402, 1406, 1407. A child of unknown parentage who is found in the United States while under the age of five is a citizen unless it is shown before the child reaches the age of twenty-one that the child was not born in the U.S. *Id.* § 1401(f).

2. 8 U.S.C. §§ 1401(c), 1401(d), 1401(e), 1401(g). The citizen parent must have met residency requirements that are specified in the law for a child born abroad to become a citizen at birth. *See also* Child Citizenship Act of 2000, Pub. L. No. 106-395, 114 Stat. 1631 (2000) (providing for automatic conferral of citizenship upon foreign-born children whose biological or adoptive parent is a citizen, when certain conditions are met).

Additional requirements must be met when a child is born abroad to a citizen father and noncitizen mother who are not married to each other. That child becomes a citizen at birth only if a blood relationship between the child and the father is established, the father agrees in writing to provide financial support for the child until the child reaches the age of eighteen, and one of the following happens before the child turns eighteen: the child is legitimated under the laws of the child's place of residence or domicile, the father acknowledges paternity in writing and under oath, or paternity is established by a court. If the child's mother is the citizen, the child is eligible for citizenship upon birth, regardless of the father's citizenship or willingness to acknowledge paternity. 8 U.S.C. § 1409. *See also* Tuan Anh Nguyen v. INS, 533 U.S. 53 (2001) (holding that it is constitutionally permissible to make this distinction between biological mothers and biological fathers).

3. 8 U.S.C. § 1408. A U.S. national owes allegiance to the United States but does not have all the rights and privileges of citizenship.

naturalizing—that is, by successfully applying for citizenship.[4] The law makes no distinction between naturalized citizens and citizens by birth; the same rights and privileges apply to each.

The term *immigrant* refers to any noncitizen who is in the United States with the intention of remaining indefinitely.[5] A noncitizen who is in the United States temporarily—such as a tourist, a business traveler, or a student with a temporary visa—is not considered an immigrant, but a visitor. The term *nonimmigrant* is often used to describe noncitizens in this category.

Federal immigration law establishes several different categories of immigrants who may lawfully enter and remain in the United States. These include lawful permanent residents, refugees, persons seeking asylum in the United States ("asylees"), and others. Lawful permanent residents have "green cards," officially known as Alien Registration Receipt Cards, Permanent Resident Cards, or Form I-551. In the past, green cards were green in color, but that is no longer the case. Today, a green card looks similar to a driver's license. Some immigrants who are legally in the United States do not have green cards, but they should have some other form of official documentation.

Some immigrants are in the United States without legal authorization. These immigrants are usually referred to as *undocumented immigrants* or *illegal aliens*.

4. Children do not apply for naturalization in the same manner as adults. Naturalized parents may apply for a certificate of citizenship for a child under the age of eighteen if both parents are naturalized, the only surviving parent (or the custodial parent if the parents are divorced) is naturalized, or, if the child is born out of wedlock, the child has not been legitimated and the mother is naturalized. For a person eighteen years of age or older to be eligible to naturalize, in most cases he or she must have been a lawful permanent resident of the United States for five years (three years if married to and living with a U.S. citizen for at least three years or serving in the armed forces for at least three years), and have resided in the U.S. for most of that time. The person must also be of good moral character, must demonstrate a basic understanding of the English language and the fundamentals of U.S. government and history, and must take an oath of allegiance to the United States. 8 U.S.C. §§ 1427, 1423, 1448.

5. The law uses the term *alien,* a term that many consider to be offensive and less accurate than *noncitizen* or *immigrant*.

When an immigrant gives birth to a child in the United States, the child is a citizen, even though the mother is not. This is an important point, because the child may be eligible for benefits and services for which his or her immigrant parent does not qualify.

Some immigrants may believe that having a child in the United States changes their own citizenship or immigration status. It does not. The mother's immigration status remains the same after she gives birth to a citizen child—so, for example, if she was undocumented, she remains undocumented and without legal authority to be in the U.S.

ARE IMMIGRANTS ELIGIBLE TO ATTEND PUBLIC SCHOOLS?

Public schools must enroll students without regard to their citizenship or immigration status. Even undocumented immigrants are eligible to attend public schools. In 1982, the United States Supreme Court ruled that it is unconstitutional to deny public education to undocumented immigrant children or to require them to pay tuition when the schools are free to citizen children.[6] Of course, public schools may require immigrant children to meet other enrollment criteria that are applied to *all* children without regard to citizenship, such as minimum and maximum age requirements.

ARE IMMIGRANTS ELIGIBLE TO RECEIVE SERVICES FROM OTHER PUBLIC AGENCIES?

Immigrants are eligible to receive many benefits and services from public agencies, but not as many as citizens. Some benefits and services are avail-

6. Plyler v. Doe, 457 U.S. 202 (1982). In North Carolina, the right to a free public education is guaranteed by the state constitution. N.C. Const. art. I, § 15 and art. X, § 2(1); *see also* Leandro v. State, 346 N.C. 336, 488 S.E.2d 249 (1997) (holding that the right to education guaranteed by the constitution "is a right to a sound basic education").

able to all immigrants, regardless of whether they are documented, but some are available only to those who meet the federal Welfare Reform Act's[7] definition of *qualified alien*. Furthermore, some benefits and services are available only to those who meet the qualified alien definition *and* have been in the United States for at least five years.

The main categories of immigrants who are considered *qualified aliens* are lawful permanent residents, refugees, political and religious asylees, and immigrants classified as Cuban/Haitian entrants or Amerasian immigrants.[8] Any noncitizen who does not meet the definition of qualified alien is considered a *nonqualified alien*[9] for the purpose of determining eligibility for benefits. A person who is a nonqualified alien is not necessarily an illegal or undocumented immigrant. Undocumented immigrants fall into the nonqualified alien category, but so do several categories of noncitizens who are lawfully in the United States—such as nonimmigrants with temporary visas and persons who have applied for asylum but have not yet been granted it.

7. The official title of the welfare reform law is the Personal Responsibility and Work Opportunity Reconciliation Act of 1996, Pub. L. No. 104-193, 110 Stat. 2105 (codified as amended in scattered sections of 8 U.S.C. and 42 U.S.C.) (hereafter Welfare Reform Act).

8. Other immigrants who fit into the *qualified alien* definition are immigrants granted "withholding of deportation" status (that is, noncitizens who ordinarily would be deported, but the U.S. attorney general has determined that they would be subject to persecution if they were required to return to their home countries), persons who have been "paroled" into the U.S. for at least one year (that is, persons who ordinarily would not be allowed to enter the U.S. but have been allowed to enter temporarily for humanitarian, medical, or legal reasons), immigrants who have been present in the U.S. since before April 1, 1980, as "conditional entrants" under federal immigration laws, and certain immigrants who have been battered or victims of a severe form of trafficking under the Trafficking Victims Protection Act.

9. The Welfare Reform Act does not use the term *nonqualified alien*, but refers to "aliens who are not qualified aliens." In the absence of an official shorthand term for this group, different terms have emerged, including *not-qualified aliens* and *unqualified aliens*. *Nonqualified alien* is used here because it appears to be the most commonly used term.

WHICH BENEFITS AND SERVICES ARE AVAILABLE
TO WHICH CATEGORIES OF IMMIGRANTS?

It is impossible to address immigrant eligibility for *all* benefits and services provided by all public agencies in North Carolina. Each agency must make some determinations about immigrant eligibility on its own, according to guidance established in the federal welfare reform law and federal agency interpretations.[10] This section describes eligibility for several major benefits or services that may be of particular relevance to pregnant or parenting minors.

Services Provided by Local Health Departments
Health Care
Immigrant minors are eligible for health care services provided through the local health department, regardless of whether they are docu-mented or meet the definition of qualified alien. Among the services immigrant minors may receive are family planning, prenatal care, diagnosis and treatment of sexually transmitted diseases, immunizations for them-selves and their children, and well-child care for their children.[11] Most health departments in North Carolina provide all these services.

Some of the health care services for which immigrant minors are eligible have fees. In some cases, an immigrant minor may be eligible for a service

10. For more information about the federal law and federal agency interpretations, see Jill D. Moore, *Immigrants' Access to Public Benefits: Who Remains Eligible for What?*, 65 POPULAR GOV'T, Fall 1999, at 22 (out of print, but available on the Internet at http://ncinfo.iog.unc.edu/pubs/electronicversions/pg/f99-2232.pdf). The National Immigration Law Center has prepared a very useful table that summarizes immigrant eligibility for federal programs. The table is available on the Internet at http://www.nilc.org/immspbs/special/Ovrvw_Imm_Elig_Fed_Pgms_4.03.pdf.

11. *See* Welfare Reform Act § 401(b) (making immunizations and communicable disease control services exceptions to the general rule that a person must be a citizen or qualified alien to receive benefits); Personal Responsibility and Work Opportunity Reconciliation Act of 1996 (PRWORA): Interpretation of Federal Public Benefit, 63 Fed. Reg. 41,657 (Aug. 4, 1998) (determining federally funded programs such as prenatal care may be provided to immigrants without respect to their immigration status).

but not eligible for Medicaid or another program that would pay for it. (Immigrant eligibility for Medicaid is discussed in the section on eligibility for social services, below.) However, some significant services are provided by local health departments at no cost. These include diagnosis and treatment of sexually transmitted diseases and immunizations that are required by law for school attendance.[12] Other services have "sliding-scale" fees that are based on what the patient can afford to pay. For example, there is a sliding-scale fee for family planning services, and minors are placed on the scale according to their *own* income, not their parents' income.[13] As a result, most minors are classified as "zero pay" and receive the services without charge.

Some difficult issues may arise when an immigrant minor who needs health care is in the U.S. without her parents. Some significant services may be provided to minors upon their own consent, including family planning services, prenatal care, and diagnosis and treatment of sexually transmitted diseases.[14] But what if a minor needs health care to which she cannot consent on her own—say, for a strep throat, or an ear infection? Health care providers may be reluctant to treat her for such conditions. However, North Carolina law may permit the treatment, depending upon the circumstances. For example, there may be someone other than a parent who may consent to her care, such as a person who is acting in loco parentis for the minor. (If there is no such person, the minor may be a neglected or dependent juvenile in need of child protective services.) In the absence of anyone with legal authority to consent to the minor's care, a health care provider may still provide treatment in an emergency, or in a nonemergency situation if her

12. N.C. Gen. Stat. § 130A-144(e) (hereafter G.S.) (sexually transmitted diseases); G.S. 130A-153(a) (immunizations).

13. N.C. Division of Public Health, *North Carolina Statewide Family Planning, Maternity and Child Health Programs (Title X and HMHC Funds) Patient Fee Policies for Local Health Agencies* (undated, but provided to author by N.C. Division of Public Health in July 2003) (on file with author).

14. G.S. 90-21.5. For complete information about minors' access to these types of care, see Anne Dellinger and Arlene M. Davis, Health Care for Pregnant Adolescents: A Legal Guide (Chapel Hill, N.C.: Institute of Government 2001), available at www.adolescentpregnancy.unc.edu.

parents cannot be located or contacted with reasonable diligence during the time within which the minor needs the treatment, or in specified other circumstances.[15]

Women, Infants, and Children Program

The Women, Infants, & Children Program (WIC)[16] provides supplemental foods, nutrition education, and other forms of support for low-income pregnant and postpartum women, infants, and young children. Any immigrant, regardless of whether she is a qualified alien or is legally in the U.S., may be eligible for WIC benefits. So long as she meets the usual eligibility criteria for WIC (for example, income eligibility criteria), her immigration status is not relevant to her eligibility for benefits.[17]

Benefits and Services Administered by Local Departments of Social Services

Temporary Assistance for Needy Families

Temporary Assistance for Needy Families (TANF), also known as the "Work First" program in North Carolina, provides financial assistance and other services to low-income families with children. To be eligible for TANF, an immigrant must (1) satisfy the usual criteria for eligibility for TANF (for example, income eligibility criteria), (2) fit within the definition of qualified

15. G.S. 90-21.1; *see also* Anne Dellinger and Arlene M. Davis, HEALTH CARE FOR PREGNANT ADOLESCENTS: A LEGAL GUIDE (Chapel Hill, N.C.: Institute of Government 2001). A second opinion is usually required before a provider may perform surgery on a minor without first obtaining her parents' consent. *See* G.S. 90-21.3.

16. Local WIC programs may be administered by an agency other than the local health department, but all local health departments are equipped to make an appropriate referral to individuals who call to inquire about WIC.

17. Welfare Reform Act § 742 states that nothing in the Welfare Reform Act shall prohibit or require a state to provide services to a person who is not a citizen or qualified alien under several programs, including WIC. The U.S. Department of Agriculture has interpreted that provision to mean that a state must affirmatively elect not to provide WIC benefits to nonqualified aliens before it may deny the benefits. North Carolina has not done so.

alien, and (3) have been in the United States with the status of qualified alien for at least five years.[18]

Medicaid

Medicaid is a public insurance program that pays for health care for designated categories of low-income persons, including pregnant women and children. To be eligible for regular Medicaid benefits, an immigrant must satisfy the usual criteria for eligibility for Medicaid (for example, income eligibility criteria) and fit within the definition of qualified alien. Most immigrants who entered the United States after August 22, 1996, are also subject to a five-year waiting period.[19] A pregnant immigrant minor will qualify for regular Medicaid benefits only if she meets all those criteria. An immigrant minor's child may qualify for regular Medicaid, even if the mother does not. If the child was born in the U.S., the child is a citizen and needs only to satisfy the usual criteria for eligibility for Medicaid. The child's mother's immigration status is irrelevant.

Emergency Medicaid eligibility is different from regular Medicaid. All immigrants who meet the financial and other eligibility criteria are eligible for emergency Medicaid, regardless of whether they are qualified aliens, and

18. *See* Welfare Reform Act § 403 (requiring immigrant applicants for "federal means-tested public benefits" to be qualified aliens and to satisfy a five-year waiting period) and Personal Responsibility and Work Opportunity Reconciliation Act of 1996 (PRWORA): Interpretation of "Federal Means-Tested Public Benefit," 62 Fed. Reg. 45,256 (Aug. 26, 1997) (concluding that TANF is a federal means-tested public benefit).

19. *See* Welfare Reform Act § 403 (requiring immigrant applicants for "federal means-tested public benefits" to be qualified aliens and to satisfy a five-year waiting period) and Personal Responsibility and Work Opportunity Reconciliation Act of 1996 (PRWORA): Interpretation of "Federal Means-Tested Public Benefit," 62 Fed. Reg. 45,256 (Aug. 26, 1997) (concluding that Medicaid is a federal means-tested public benefit). Immigrants who entered the United States before August 22, 1996, are not subject to the five-year waiting period. Certain categories of qualified aliens, such as refugees and asylees, are exempted from the waiting period.

regardless of whether they are legally in the United States.[20] Among other things, emergency Medicaid covers health care services for labor and delivery. A pregnant immigrant minor who is otherwise eligible for Medicaid benefits therefore should qualify for emergency Medicaid to cover her childbirth expenses, regardless of her citizenship or immigration status.[21]

Finally, any pregnant immigrant may be granted presumptive eligibility for Medicaid by a qualified provider, such as a local health department, for services such as prenatal care, regardless of whether she is documented or a qualified alien. Under presumptive eligibility, a pregnant minor's health care provider can certify her for up to two months of coverage if the provider determines from preliminary information that the minor may meet Medicaid's income eligibility criteria. Once the presumptive eligibility period expires, the pregnant minor will not be able to continue to receive Medicaid unless she has applied for regular Medicaid and is eligible to receive it.

20. *See* Welfare Reform Act § 401(b) (making emergency Medicaid an exception to the general rule that a person must be a citizen or qualified alien to receive benefits).

21. However, if the minor is a noncitizen who is in the U.S. on an unexpired temporary visa, her application for emergency Medicaid may be denied. To be eligible for Medicaid, an applicant must be a resident of the state in which he or she applies. To be considered a resident, a person must live in the state with the intention of remaining here permanently or for an indefinite period of time. 42 C.F.R. § 435.403(i)(1)(i). If an applicant does not meet the residency requirement, the application will be denied. In 2002, the North Carolina Court of Appeals held that the state Division of Medical Assistance properly denied emergency Medicaid to a nonimmigrant woman who gave birth while in the U.S. on an unexpired tourist visa, on the ground that the woman could not satisfy the residency requirement. The Division maintained that the woman could not meet the residency requirement since she was legally obligated to leave the United States before her visa expired. The woman countered that she satisfied the residency requirement because she intended to overstay her visa and remain in North Carolina indefinitely (though unlawfully). The court of appeals acknowledged the woman's stated intention but concluded that her unexpired temporary tourist visa called that intention into doubt. Okale v. N.C. Dep't of Health and Human Services, 153 N.C. App. 475, 570 S.E.2d 741 (2002). This ruling does not appear to support a denial of emergency Medicaid to an undocumented immigrant, whose assertion of an intention to remain here indefinitely would not be contradicted by her own official paperwork.

N.C. Health Choice

N.C. Health Choice (State Children's Health Insurance Program) is a public health insurance program for children whose family income is too high to qualify for Medicaid but still less than 200 percent of the federal poverty level. To be eligible for Health Choice, an immigrant must satisfy the usual criteria for eligibility for Health Choice (for example, income eligibility criteria) and fit within the definition of qualified alien. If the immigrant entered the United States after August 22, 1996, it is likely that he or she must also satisfy a five-year waiting period. However, Health Choice does not cover maternity care, regardless of the minor's immigration status. An immigrant minor's child may be eligible for this program, if the usual eligibility criteria for Health Choice are satisfied and the child is *either* a U.S. citizen *or* a qualified alien who has satisfied the waiting period (if applicable).

Child Protective Services

Any immigrant—regardless of qualified or legal status—is eligible for child protective services (CPS).[22] Citizenship or immigration status is not a legitimate consideration in deciding whether to report an abused, neglected, or dependent minor to CPS; nor is it a legitimate consideration for DSS in deciding whether to investigate the report or substantiate abuse or neglect. A pregnant or parenting immigrant minor may need child protective services herself, or her child may need the services.

Emergency Medical Care

All persons are eligible for transportation by ambulances and other emergency medical services, without regard to their citizenship or immigration

---

22. *See* Welfare Reform Act § 401(b) (making community programs necessary for the protection of life and safety an exception to the general rule that a person must be a citizen or qualified alien to receive benefits) and Specification of Community Programs Necessary for Protection of Life and Safety under Welfare Reform Legislation, 61 Fed. Reg. 45,985 (Aug. 30, 1996) (specifically designating child protective services as a community program necessary for the protection of life and safety).

status.[23] Furthermore, a federal law designed to forbid hospitals from "patient dumping" requires most hospitals with emergency departments to provide certain emergency care to any patient who seeks it, including care for a pregnant woman in labor.[24]

WILL PUBLIC AGENCIES ASK ABOUT IMMIGRATION STATUS OR ATTEMPT TO VERIFY WHETHER SOMEONE IS LEGALLY IN THE U.S.?

An immigrant minor may be reluctant to seek public benefits or services for which she is eligible if she fears she will be asked about her immigration status. But public agencies must not ask about or attempt to verify a client's citizenship or immigration status unless it is required to deny the benefit or service to some or all noncitizens.[25] As explained above, in some cases public agencies must deny services or benefits to a potential client who is an immigrant if she is not a qualified alien, or if she is a qualified alien who is subject to the five-year waiting period. In order to determine that services or benefits must be denied, at some point applicants must be asked to verify their citizenship or immigration status. However, there are specific steps that public agencies must follow *before* they inquire about citizenship or immigration status.

23. *See* Welfare Reform Act § 401(b) and Specification of Community Programs Necessary for Protection of Life and Safety under Welfare Reform Legislation, 61 Fed. Reg. 45,985 (Aug. 30, 1996).

24. Emergency Medical Treatment and Active Labor Act, 42 U.S.C. § 1395dd.

25. This conclusion and the steps that are outlined in this section are derived from a U.S. Department of Justice guidance document. Interim Guidance on Verification of Citizenship, Qualified Alien Status and Eligibility under Title VI of the Personal Responsibility and Work Opportunity Reconciliation Act of 1996, 62 Fed. Reg. 61,344 (Nov. 17, 1997). For more information, see Alison Brown, *When Should Agencies Inquire About Immigration Status?*, 65 POPULAR GOV'T, Fall 1999, at 29 (out of print but available on the Internet at http://ncinfo.iog.unc.edu/pubs/electronicversions/pg/agencies.htm).

First, the agency must determine whether the program or benefit the client wishes to receive is one that is available to all eligible applicants or if it must be denied to certain classes of immigrants. For example, TANF is a benefit program that must be denied to certain immigrants, while communicable disease control services may not be denied.

Second, the agency staff must determine whether the person seeking the service or benefit meets all other eligibility criteria—for example, financial or categorical criteria—before assessing whether the person meets the citizenship or immigration criteria.

Third, if the person has satisfied the other eligibility criteria, agency staff must verify whether the person is a U.S. citizen, a U.S. national, or a qualified alien. This step should never be reached if the benefit or service is not contingent upon the person's citizenship or immigration status. Also, if a person is applying for benefits on behalf of another person, the agency should verify only the status of the person who is to receive the benefit. For example, if a minor mother is applying for Medicaid for her child, only the child's status should be assessed. If the child was born in the United States, the agency should treat the child as a citizen, regardless of whether the parents are citizens.

Finally, if the person is a qualified alien, the provider should determine if additional restrictions—such as the five-year waiting period for Medicaid—apply to the services that are sought. If additional restrictions apply, the agency must determine whether they are satisfied.

IS LANGUAGE ASSISTANCE AVAILABLE TO MINORS WITH LIMITED ENGLISH PROFICIENCY?

Public schools and other public agencies that receive federal financial assistance must provide language assistance to students or clients who have limited English proficiency. A person is considered limited-English-proficient (LEP) if she cannot speak, write, read, or understand the English language sufficiently well to interact effectively with service providers. Some LEP minors are immigrants, but some are citizens. This legal requirement is derived from Title VI of the federal Civil Rights Act. [26]

Compliance with this legal requirement is overseen by different federal agencies. For example, compliance in the public schools is overseen by the Department of Education, while compliance in local health departments and social services agencies is overseen by the Department of Health and Human Services. The federal agencies are required to publish guidance documents explaining what the language assistance requirements are and how agencies that receive federal financial assistance must comply.[27] Because the guidance documents are published by different agencies, they are not identical, even though they have the same legal foundation in Title VI. As a result, the guidance provided to schools is different from the guidance provided to human services agencies. For example, the guidance published by the federal Department of Education focuses on LEP students' needs in the classroom, while the guidance published by the Department of Health and Human Services focuses more on clients' rights. But this does not mean that the legal obligations are completely different for schools and human services agencies. The intent of Title VI is to prohibit discrimination. If a school's or other agency's actions have the effect of discriminating against LEP persons, a federal oversight agency or a court could conclude that the agency has violated Title VI, even if the agency otherwise complies with any applicable guidance documents.

---

26. 42 U.S.C. § 2001d. Title VI prohibits recipients of federal financial assistance from denying benefits to a person or excluding a person from participating in a program or service because of the person's race, color, or national origin. Title VI does not explicitly mention language assistance or prohibit discrimination on the basis of limited English proficiency. However, in 1974, the U.S. Supreme Court held that failure to provide language assistance to LEP students in a public school violated Title VI, because it had a disparate impact on students based on their national origin and denied non-English-speaking students a meaningful opportunity to participate in the educational program. Lau v. Nichols, 414 U.S. 563 (1974).

27. *See* President's Executive Order No. 13,166, 65 Fed. Reg. 50,119 (August 16, 2000) (requiring federal agencies to develop Title VI guidance for recipients of the agencies' financial assistance).

In the face of incomplete guidance on how to comply with Title VI, a school or public agency can best serve its LEP students or clients by keeping them in mind at all times, especially when developing forms or other written materials containing information they need to know, or policies or procedures that will affect them.

Language Assistance in Public Schools

Federal and state laws require public schools to provide language assistance to LEP students. A 1974 U.S. Supreme Court case held that failure to assist LEP students violates Title VI of the federal Civil Rights Act.[28] The federal Equal Educational Opportunities Act requires schools to take "appropriate action" to overcome language barriers that impede students' equal participation in instructional programs.[29] In general, this means that public schools must identify and evaluate LEP students and provide an educational program that helps those students overcome language barriers.[30]

28. Lau v. Nichols, 414 U.S. 563 (1974).

29. 20 U.S.C. § 1703(f).

30. *See* U.S. Department of Education Office for Civil Rights, *The Provision of an Equal Education Opportunity to Limited-English Proficient Students* (August 2000), available on the Internet at http://www.ed.gov/about/offices/list/ocr/eeolep/index.html. The Department of Education's guidance on Title VI compliance for LEP students is limited to the instructional context and does not address whether schools might have other obligations to LEP students or their parents. For example, unlike the guidance offered to human services agencies by the U.S. Department of Health and Human Services, the Department of Education's guidance does not specifically address the translation of important documents into other languages. Nevertheless, it is possible that a court could hold that Title VI requires schools to undertake this or other steps to ensure accurate communications with LEP students or parents.

Even in the absence of a clear legal obligation, schools should make every effort to communicate with LEP students and parents in a language they can understand about vital issues such as students' rights (e.g., in the case of suspension or expulsion), available benefits (e.g., free or reduced-price lunch), and safety (e.g., emergency procedures).

In North Carolina, state regulations require local education agencies to adopt programs for LEP students that "have a reasonable chance of allowing [those] students to progress in school."[31] A local education agency may adopt an English as a Second Language (ESL) program, provide bilingual instruction, or adopt another program that adapts instruction to meet the needs of LEP students.

Language Assistance in Public Human Services Agencies

LEP minors who seek assistance from public human services agencies, such as the local health department or department of social services, are entitled to receive language assistance from those agencies. There are a number of things public human services agencies must do to ensure their compliance with federal laws governing language assistance.[32] This section summarizes only a few of the most significant requirements.

Public human services agencies must provide oral interpretation services for LEP clients. *Public human services agencies must never charge LEP clients for language assistance or require clients to provide or arrange for their own interpreters.* In most cases, agencies should not use a client's friend

31. 16 NCAC 6D.0106.

32. In 2002, the federal Department of Health and Human Services determined that the North Carolina Department of Health and Human Services was not providing adequate assistance to LEP clients and thus was in violation of Title VI of the federal Civil Rights Act. The state and federal departments entered into a compliance agreement in which the state agreed to develop a language assistance policy and to require local human services agencies to develop policies as well. The compliance agreement and the N.C. DHHS Title VI Language Access Policy (May 2003) are on file with the author. The compliance agreement was based on policy guidance that the U.S. DHHS issued in 2000. Title VI of the Civil Rights Act of 1964; Policy Guidance on the Prohibition Against National Origin Discrimination As it Affects Persons With Limited English Proficiency, 65 Fed. Reg. 52,762 (Aug. 30, 2000). The policy guidance was recently revised. See Guidance to Federal Financial Assistance Recipients Regarding Title VI Prohibition Against National Origin Discrmination Affecting Limited English Proficient Persons, 68 Fed. Reg. 47,311 (Aug. 8, 2003).

or family member as an interpreter. Before using a friend or family member, agency staff should inform the LEP client that the agency will arrange for an alternative interpreter at no cost. If the LEP client declines the offer and asks to use the friend or family member instead, the agency may use that person *only if* it determines that doing so does not compromise the effectiveness of the service or violate the LEP client's confidentiality. It may be particularly important for a pregnant LEP minor to understand that she cannot be required to use her parent or partner as her interpreter.

Written materials that are routinely provided in English to agency clients and to the public must also be available in other languages that the agency encounters frequently, such as Spanish. It is particularly important that "vital" documents be translated. These include documents such as applications, consent forms, letters with important information about benefit eligibility or participation in a program, notices regarding reduction, denial, or termination of services or benefits, and notices advising LEP clients that free language assistance is available to them.

Finally, public human services agencies must give LEP clients notice of their right to free language assistance. The notice must be given in a language the LEP person can understand.